PLAY THE BALL WHERE
THE MONKEY DROPS IT

PLAY THE BALL WHERE THE MONKEY DROPS IT

*Why We Suffer and
How We Can Hope*

Gregory Knox Jones

HarperSanFrancisco
A Division of HarperCollins*Publishers*

HarperCollins books may be purchased for educational, business, or sales promotional use. For information please write: Special Markets Department, HarperCollins Publishers, Inc., 10 East 53rd Street, New York, NY 10022.

HarperCollins Web site: http://www.harpercollins.com
HarperCollins®, 🕮®, and HarperSanFrancisco™ are trademarks of HarperCollins Publishers, Inc.

FIRST EDITION

Library of Congress Cataloging-in-Publication Data
Jones, Gregory Knox
Play the ball where the monkey drops it : why we suffer and how we can hope / Gregory Knox Jones. — 1st ed.
p. cm.
Includes bibliographical references.
ISBN 0–688–17142–7 (cloth : alk. paper)
1. Suffering—Religious aspects—Christianity. 2. Theodicy. I. Title.
BT732.7.J665 2001
231'.8—dc21
00-143874

01 02 03 04 05 ❖ QF 10 9 8 7 6 5 4 3 2 1

For Camilla

CONTENTS

Foreword	ix
Acknowledgments	xvii
Introduction	xix
PART ONE: No Protective Bubble	1
CHAPTER ONE: Play the Ball Where the Monkey Drops It	3
CHAPTER TWO: Why Is There Such Widespread Suffering?	12
PART TWO: Describing God	33
CHAPTER THREE: God Feels Every Ounce of Our Pain	35
CHAPTER FOUR: An Open Future (or God Knows All Possible Futures)	43
CHAPTER FIVE: Persuasive Power	54
CHAPTER SIX: "I'm Praying for a Sweet Potato"	62
CHAPTER SEVEN: The Power of Transformation	77
PART THREE: Detecting God's Voice in Our Lives	89
CHAPTER EIGHT: The Whispers of God	91
CHAPTER NINE: Life After Death?	113

CHAPTER TEN: Moving from Grief to Cherished
Memories   130
CHAPTER ELEVEN: Live a Rich Life!   148

Conclusion   159
Notes   163

Foreword

I very much enjoyed reading Dr. Jones's book because I have struggled with the same questions. I experienced tears and laughter while reading it, which tells me this book truly speaks of the nature of life. The subtitle reads, "Why We Suffer and How We Can Hope." From my experience, as a surgeon, I have learned that we suffer when the pain we experience has no meaning and we find it impossible to be hopeful when we fail to understand the nature of life. As a surgeon I asked many of the same questions this book confronts. I wondered why life had to be so painful and cruel. I watched children die of cancer and suffer permanent injuries due to accidents or abuse. None of it made any sense. I was always asking why but no one answered. *Play the Ball Where the Monkey Drops It* provides new insights into this age-old problem.

My medical education did not deal with questions of this type. We were trained to care for diseases, not people. Spiritual issues were not discussed in medical school nor during my training.

I wondered and questioned but received no answers that made any sense. Why would God create a world with all these afflictions and difficulties? I wondered how Abraham could say yes to a God who asked him to sacrifice his own son. I studied religions to find answers. Judaism tells us disease is not a punishment from God but a loss of health and we are to look for treatment that will heal us and cure us. I now ask people, "If you lose your car keys, does God want you to walk home?" When they laugh I say, "Then if you'd look for your car keys, look for your health too." The Muslim faith leads one to believe that within the disease is a gift; that our afflictions can be our teachers, but why do we have to learn the hard way?

The Reverend Billy Graham was asked in his newspaper column by a reader, "Does God want me to have cancer?" He answered, "Not necessarily." His answer bothered me and he didn't answer my letter to him about God's forgiveness.

He went on to say the disease could bring you closer to God. That may be, but I think we all have enough problems to do that already and God doesn't have to hit us over the head to get our attention. Over the years, I have noticed that many Roman Catholics, as well as those from fundamentalist religious backgrounds, have been made to feel guilty for the problems they encounter. Their faith has taught them: "When you break the rules you deserve to be punished."

The problem is God handed down ten commandments, along with his mercy and justice. The people who have come after our Creator have added many rules God had nothing to do with. In the mid-1800s the pope declared that good Catholics would not vaccinate their children against smallpox because God decided who would contract smallpox. Thus, if you vaccinated your child and the child developed cancer, it was believed to be evidence that God was punishing you and you deserved to die of cancer. The rules have changed since those days, but what about the guilt bestowed upon those who lived at that time and the guilt they are living with today for being imperfect? We are all perfectly imperfect children of God.

When I speak to large audiences I ask, Is life fair? The resounding answer is no. I then say, "It must be fair. You're all complaining."

Yes, life is fair but it is also very difficult. Why? That is what *Play the Ball Where the Monkey Drops It* and my experience have sought to answer for us. Part of the answer is found in living a more meaningful life. When our pain has meaning it is tolerable and controllable.

My mother's answer, which I never felt happy with as a teenager, was "It was meant to be. God is redirecting you.

Something good will come of this." I spent a good deal of time talking to God because my mother didn't seem very helpful, but as life went on I discovered the wisdom of her words.

Yes, many afflictions and difficulties led me on new paths that ultimately were very rewarding. So I opened my mind and view of life and learned to accept many events in a more serene manner, not knowing the effect they would have on my future.

What is a blessing? Why does the Bible tell us that after God created everything, God saw that it was "good." But in the Bible, after God created man, that statement does not appear. The problem is that the Hebrew word *Tov* is translated too loosely. The word *good* has too many meanings in the English language.

The word *Tov* should be translated as "complete." So human beings are not complete. And what is a blessing? Anything that helps us to find completion. To fill the void. Some of those things are painful and difficult for us to experience, but if we become more complete we will find that life does become more meaningful, easier to understand, and easier to survive. We have to learn why we are here and who our Lord is. I have learned that if we have the right Lord when times are difficult, our Lord's words and prayer are a resource.

The fact that we have free will creates problems but also makes life meaningful. The Garden of Eden is boring.

I have been there as an outside consultant to The Board of Directors of Heaven. Everyone loves you. The weather is great, etc., and it drives you nuts after a while. On earth if someone loves you and we have a nice day it means something because there are other options.

Despite all of life's difficulties I believe in a loving, intelligent, energetic, conscious Creator. I believe we are here to learn much as we did in school and that we are more than just physical bodies. So we live more than once and continue our education until we reach enlightenment. *Play the Ball Where the Monkey Drops It* can save you a lot of hard-fought learning and move you up several classes with its wisdom. Better to become strong enough to not break or learn how to utilize the break to expand, which reading this book will accomplish, than to have to become strong at the broken places. Before I tell you a story that taught me what I needed to know as a surgeon about the big question we are confronting, let me tell you about three plaques that sit over God's desk and should help you relax.

One says, "Don't feel totally, personally, irrevocably, eternally responsible for everything. That's my job." Second, "Everything you remember, I forget. Everything you forget, I remember," and third, "If you go around saying, 'I've got a miserable life,' I'll show you what miserable really is. If you go around saying, 'I've got a wonderful life,' I'll show you what wonderful really is."

What taught me about why there is pain in the world was the following experience. When I asked my father, the hospital chaplain, and others, I received these answers: "To learn lessons," "God knows," "Why not?" "Who knows?" "That's life," and "I don't know." They didn't leave me satisfied or feeling enlightened. My mother, always the wise one, told me that nature had all the answers, just as the Bible tells us, and perhaps a walk in the woods would help me to find an answer.

Many things happened on my walk to teach me the lessons I needed to learn. It was winter so I put on my hat and jacket and started off. Shortly after entering the woods I noted a holly tree had fallen across my path.

When I went to pull it up I cut my hand on its pointed leaves. I put my gloves on and finally moved the tree out of the way. Further on I saw five boys all tangled together lying on the ground in the snow. I asked them why they didn't get up and they said they were so tangled they didn't know which part belonged to whom and were afraid they'd break something if they moved. I removed a shoe from one of the boys, took a stick, and jabbed it into his foot. He yelled, "Ow" and I said, "That's your foot, now move it." I kept jabbing until all the boys were separated. I eventually learned from these incidents that emotional and physical pain are necessary for us to experience or we cannot protect ourselves, know ourselves, and respond to our needs and the needs of our loved ones.

Further along that day, I saw a duck trapped in a bush with its head caught in the plastic from a six-pack. I went over, gently freed the duck, held it up, and off it flew. I was waiting for God to give me another message but heard nothing so I kept walking. Maybe my mother was wrong about nature.

At the end of the path I saw a deer sprawled on the ice of a frozen pond. She kept slipping and sliding and couldn't get up. I went out, calmed her by feeding her some acorns, and then helped her off the ice. I expected her to run away when we got to dry land, but instead of running away, she and some other deer, that came out of the woods started walking toward me. I didn't like the look of the other deer's antlers so I started running home and could hear them running after me. When I was close enough to our house to feel safe, I turned to look at them. They stopped and we looked into one anothers eyes. There was my answer. They were thanking me for being compassionate in their time of trouble. I realized then that we are here to continue God's work and, if the world were perfect, it would simply be a magic trick with no meaning or chance for us to learn, work, and create.

We are the ones who will have to create the world I was hoping for. A world where there is evil does not respond to the person with the affliction, whether it be emotional or physical. I can now understand that God has given us work to do. I will still grieve my losses but I will use my pain to help me know myself and respond to the needs of others. That is my work as our Creator intended it to be. My question has been answered by the nature of life.

Jesus said it well: "The son of man comes not to be served but to serve and to ransom his life for the good of the many." Remember this modern parable: "We are satellite dishes, remote controls, and television screens." We have many options as to what channels we choose to tune in to. So God gives us a mind to select with, like a remote control, and a body to display what we have heard and witnessed, like a TV screen. The key is what channel are you tuning in to? What voice are you listening to? If it is the true Lord and not material things that your life is dedicated to, then you will understand the nature of life and have faith, as Abraham did. You can now say yes to your Lord when asked to live and act as a co-creator because you know your Lord has the greater good in mind, and to appreciate that good, one must also have free will, which means there will be difficulties too.

A last word of advice: If you want to live forever, love someone.

Sooner or later our bodies will all perish, but if they perish without love, which the wise declare is the only thing of permanence, of what use will they have been?

—Bernie Siegel, M.D.

⋇

Acknowledgments

Emerging from my ministry in two congregations, this book represents the evolution of my religious beliefs as I struggled with parishioners through dark periods of their lives. Many of us grew up believing that if we were faithful to God, terrible tragedies would not strike us directly. Yet, some people's actual experience of life blatantly defied this belief.

I am deeply grateful for the friends who not only shared their heartaches with me, but who had the courage to openly question why God had allowed such pain and suffering to batter their lives. Pressing me for answers, they drew me into their struggles with God and forced me to wrestle with my theology. The answers I discovered reshaped my understanding of God and enabled me to make sense of suffering while recovering genuine hope. I will be ever grateful to the members of Chester Presbyterian Church in Chester, Virginia, and First

Presbyterian Church in Lexington, Kentucky, for opening their lives to me. Most of what is found between these covers was first shared in worship with the faithful in Chester.

I am indebted to several professors at Louisville Presbyterian Seminary, especially John McClure who helped me become a better communicator and Burton Cooper whose wisdom and guidance stimulated my thinking and helped me more than he will ever know.

My good friends Larry Reed and Bob Pierce deserve thanks for reading an early draft of my manuscript. Their suggestions greatly enhanced my work.

I am grateful for my enthusiastic agent, Carol Roth, for finding the right publisher, and to Joann Davis, my first editor, whose sound advice and expertise improved the organization of the finished product, and to John Loudon, my editor at HarperSanFrancisco for his commitment and guidance.

The support and encouragement of my children and parents is a blessing beyond words, and if not for the love and sacrifices of my wife, Camilla, this book would not be in your hands. There were several times when I was ready to give up trying to bring all of these ideas together in the form of a book, but Camilla gave me the necessary boost to see it through to completion. I cannot imagine a better companion for life.

Introduction

"I need a huge favor," were the first words out of Judy's mouth when I answered the telephone. "Some friends of mine desperately need a minister."

Her friends, a twenty-something couple, were experiencing every parent's dreaded nightmare. Their seven-month-old child had died and Judy was calling to ask if I could do the funeral.

Three days later a stark image was etched into my mind forever. It was the sight of these young parents carrying a tiny white casket to a cavity in the earth. They appeared catatonic as they trudged through the frozen grass, carrying their precious child for the final time. Their feet were heavy, each step more arduous than the last, and they kept wishing they would awaken from a sleepy stupor to discover it was all a horrible dream. But this was no mere nightmare. Their infant son was dead and they struggled to understand why this overwhelming tragedy had struck them. As I said the final prayer and benediction, the young mother and father filled the silence with deep moans. They felt as if a nuclear device had been detonated in their souls. The devastation was massive and they struggled to make sense of their catastrophe. Had they done something wrong? Were they being punished for some offense? They pleaded with me for answers.

If God is good, then why do innocent children die? All people of faith must answer this question, and the way we answer has far-reaching implications. Our solution of this dilemma satisfies more than mere intellectual curiosity. It determines what we believe about God's involvement in our lives and what basis we have for hope. Thus it strongly influences the course our lives take.

For many years I struggled with this troublesome question. What I had been taught to believe about God simply did not square with the profound suffering experienced by my parishioners (not to mention such monstrous evils as the Holocaust). Time and again the members of my congregation would ask me why they suffered devastating losses and told me they would continue to hound me if I replied with simplistic responses such as, "We have to trust that God has a reason." My people sensed what I had been thinking for some time—some of the traditional religious answers are no longer satisfactory.

As a pastor who has served in the parish for more than

twenty years, I have been summoned to console families struggling with the loss of loved ones from cancer, suicide, and sudden accidents. I have buried young children, college students on the verge of graduation, and people in the prime of their lives. Over time, the traditional answers to unjust suffering proved to be inadequate. A fresh understanding of God gradually evolved as I faced real life tragedies and kept asking, Why would God allow this to happen? Call it an internal struggle that would not abate or call it a religious quest I could not avoid, I had no alternative but to revise my ideas about God.

It took several years, but the answers began to take shape. As I shared them with members of my congregation, they responded with enthusiasm. Many said that for the first time they understood why devastating blows could strike anyone. Even better, they were recovering a stronger sense of hope.

My answers are contained within the covers of this book, and they are for everyone whose life has been (or will be) touched by grief—which is to say all of us. I have tried to avoid using abstract language and complex explanations, but that is not to imply that the answers are always easy to embrace. Real answers to the difficult dilemmas of life are not always easy to adopt. My prayer is that what I have written will help you understand why suffering is so prevalent in our world, and how—despite its presence—you can live a genuinely hopeful life.

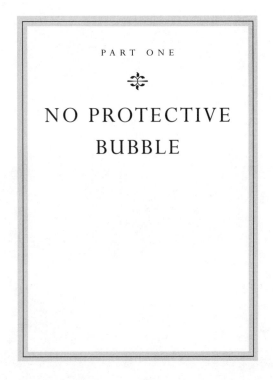

PART ONE

NO PROTECTIVE
BUBBLE

CHAPTER ONE

Play the Ball
Where the Monkey Drops It

The story is told of a golf course in India. Apparently, once the English had colonized the country and established their businesses, they yearned for recreation and decided to build a golf course in Calcutta. Golf in Calcutta presented a unique obstacle. Monkeys would drop out of the trees, scurry across the course, and seize the golf balls. The monkeys would play with the balls, tossing them here and there.

At first, the golfers tried to control the monkeys. Their first strategy was to build high fences around the fairways and greens. This approach, which seemed initially to hold much promise, was abandoned when the golfers discovered that a fence is no challenge to an ambitious monkey. Next, the golfers tried luring the monkeys away from the course. But the monkeys found nothing as amusing as watching humans go wild whenever their little white balls were disturbed. In desperation, the British began trapping the monkeys. But for every monkey they carted off, another would appear. Finally, the golfers gave in to reality and developed a rather novel ground rule: Play the ball where the monkey drops it.

As you can imagine, playing this unique way could be maddening. A beautiful drive down the center of the fairway might be picked up by a monkey and then dropped in the rough. Or the opposite could happen. A hook or slice that had produced a miserable lie might be flung onto the fairway. It did not take long before the golfers realized that golf on this particular course was very similar to our experience of life. There are good breaks, and there are bad breaks.[1] We cannot entirely control the outcome of the game.

Some mornings you climb out of bed and everything seems perfect. You pull on the right clothes, breakfast tastes delicious, and the children are pleasant. Driving to work, you hit all the green lights, hear an inspiring story on the radio, and accomplish more than anticipated at work. The monkey drops the ball a few inches from the cup.

Other days are not nearly as kind. These are the ones people generally remember (and usually share with others). Despite a packed closet, there seems to be nothing to wear. The only item in the refrigerator is a shriveled piece of fruit, and you are forced to go without breakfast.

You cannot find your car keys, but once you do, you're stopped by every red light on the way to work. Once you arrive, the computers go down. The monkey has tossed the ball from the green into a thicket.

Sometimes there are good breaks, and sometimes there are bad breaks. They are not all beyond our control. For the student who graduates from high school with exceptional grades, the opportunity to attend any college in the country is not simply a lucky break. For the student who graduates with poor grades, having few options is not simply a bad break. Discipline and good study habits make a difference. How we apply ourselves has an impact on our lives.

However, some of the breaks in life—both good and bad—are beyond our control. Loving families, miraculous medical cures, being born in a free and prosperous country—these are some of the good breaks that simply happen.

Not long ago I experienced one of those marvelous days that make us especially mindful of the beauty and goodness of life. My morning began with visits to a couple of local hospitals. The first visit promised to be delightful because a young couple in our congregation had just given birth to their first child, a beautiful girl. The infant, Morgan Elizabeth, had been born into the world at 5:56 A.M., and less than an hour later her elated father called me with the exciting news. After finishing breakfast, I headed to the hospital, where I found the mom, dad, and grandparents gushing over their new-born—a gorgeous, healthy baby girl. They were very much aware that they were blessed by the event, and I was even more aware of how blessed Morgan Elizabeth was to be born into such a loving and supportive family.

From that hospital room bursting with joy, thankful-ness, and hope, I drove to another hospital in our area. As I traveled, I worried about what I would find at my second destination. A little seven-year-old girl in our church was undergoing surgery. Amanda's problem had developed very suddenly. Only two days earlier, the doctors had located the cause of her stomachaches and bleeding. Using one of the gifts of modern medicine, an ultrasound, the physicians had discovered a large mass the size of a softball on one of her ovaries. The doctors were uncertain whether it was benign or cancerous, and so surgery was scheduled quickly.

When I arrived at the hospital, I found a tense family in the waiting room. A nurse had already ventured out from the operating room to inform the family that the surgeon had taken a biopsy and sent it to the laboratory for testing. The physicians would wait to hear the news of the pathology report before closing the incision.

There was nothing for us to do but wait. Finally, after a very long time, a nurse came bounding out the doors with a jubilant smile lighting her face. "I have great news for you! The report came back, and it was benign. There's nothing to worry about—Amanda will be fine."

It was a glorious way to begin a day. Two families in two hospitals, two marvelous events that produced tears of joy in our eyes. Some days are like that, and life is wonderful.

But we know that life is not always so. Life is not all beauty and goodness. Bad things also happen, and some of them can be devastating. These are not the bad breaks of hitting all the red lights when you are in a hurry, or having the computers go down. These are the tragedies that alter people's lives forever.

If you have never experienced the devastation of a personal tragedy, you may find it easy to believe that God is good and is protecting you from harm. If your life has not been shattered by overwhelming grief, it may be comforting to believe that God has everything under control and will safeguard your family and close friends from innocent suffering. But what happens when your world comes crumbling down around you as you encounter suffering—unjust suffering—head on? What happens to your faith in God when you discover that there is no protective bubble around your loved ones, keeping them safe and secure?

Consider the 1995 earthquake in Kobe, Japan, where people were crushed as they slept, and hundreds of thousands were left without homes. Or the bombing of the federal building in Oklahoma City that killed 168 people, including 19 children who were innocently playing in the day-care center. Or the pathology report that comes back with the worst possible news. Or the death of a loved one at an early age.

Although it has now been several years, I can still vividly recall one crisp autumn afternoon in 1992. That was the day I entered a hospital room where a member of my congregation, Reggie Morris, was lying in bed. His wife was standing beside him, and both of them smiled and offered warm greetings. But their smiles were forced, and it was obvious that they were deeply worried. I asked Reggie why he was in the hospital.

He attempted to sound nonchalant and untroubled in his response, but he was not as convincing as he imagined. He said he began having a slight difficulty, and his doctor wanted to run a few tests. I asked him to be specific.

Reggie went on to describe the previous Tuesday morning. That day, as he was getting dressed for work, his left hand would not function properly. He couldn't button his shirt, a simple task he had performed countless times with no difficulty.

Reggie managed to get dressed and drive to his office, but later that day he began to feel ill. At the encouragement of his office mates, he headed home early. The following day, with his condition unimproved, he visited his doctor, who put him in the hospital to undergo tests. A couple of days following my visit, our worst fears were confirmed. A sizable tumor—larger than a golf ball—had attached itself to Reggie's brain, and immediate surgery was required.

It all happened so quickly. One week Reggie was enjoying life and fulfilling his responsibilities as a well-respected attorney and part-time judge; the next week he was lying in a hospital bed staring at the ceiling and pondering the greatest challenge of his life.

Reggie faced his surgery with courage, constantly reassuring his wife and four sons that everything would be all right. They surely wanted to believe him but were understandably anxious about the outcome. We all were.

The surgery was not a failure, but neither was it a success. Most of the tumor was removed, but it was impossible for the surgeon to get it all because the tumor had its tentacles embedded in Reggie's brain. The game plan now called for weekly radiation treatments. They helped, holding the tumor in check. But the body can withstand only so many doses of radiation before they produce more harm than good.

The next line of defense was chemotherapy. Reggie maintained a positive attitude despite feeling terrible much of the time. After a number of weeks of chemotherapy, Reggie had another CAT scan. The tumor had grown back as large as before.

Reggie refused to give up. He garnered strength from a higher source and underwent surgery a second time. The results? About the same as before—the doctors were unable to get the entire tumor.

Reggie and his family did everything they could. For over a year, a great number of people from our church, as well as friends and relatives, sincerely prayed for him to get well, but nothing stopped the cancer. After a long, slow deterioration, Reggie died. He was only fifty-seven years old.

For our church family, this was only the beginning. Cancer made its way into the lives of several of our members over the next few years. Connie, a longtime member with a special gift for decorating the church on festive occasions, died in her early fifties. Then Annette and Pat, two talented young women with hearts of kindness—both only forty-one years old—died in September 1997 after long struggles with breast cancer. The following year, Paula, who had a great sense of humor, died of a brain tumor before reaching her fiftieth birthday. Within a year, Linda, a gentle woman who served our church in many capacities, died of breast cancer at age forty-six. Each of these women left behind a husband and children who were devastated by their deaths.

At each of the funerals, overflow crowds jammed our sanctuary. Lodged in the minds of most who attended was one simple question: Why? Why did this happen to Reggie? To Connie? To Annette? To Pat? To Paula? To Linda?

⚜

Why Is There Such Widespread Suffering?

At one time or another, most people have asked the question, Why? Perhaps the question was prompted by the death of a friend cut down in the prime of life, or a loved one who contracted an incurable disease and died an early death. Or maybe the question arose when a classmate of your child was killed in an automobile accident, or when a neighbor died an untimely death, leaving behind a wife and young children.

My earliest memory of encountering innocent suffering was at age seven. Next door lived a family of three—a father and mother in their twenties and their son, Rod, a playmate of mine. One day when I returned home from school, my mother told me that something horrible had happened. Rod's father, a promising young attorney, had been in a plane crash. The small private plane carried five passengers, and only one person survived. It was not my friend's father. He had perished, leaving my young friend and his mother devastated.

A few years later the great baseball star Roberto Clemente died in a plane crash during the off-season. Because he was one of my heroes, his death came as a jolt. Even though I was young, I knew that something was awry in the divine scheme of things. Hadn't I been told in my Sunday school class that God would protect us and keep us from harm? What made it even harder to comprehend was that Clemente was on a mission of mercy, delivering food and supplies to earthquake victims in Nicaragua. I remember thinking, "This is unfair! It isn't right! It's the same as when Rod's father died. Why would God allow such things to happen?" Sometime early on I must have fused in my mind these two incidents. To this day, whenever I hear a reference to the great Roberto Clemente, I simultaneously remember receiving the news of the death of my next-door neighbor.

It is a rare person who has not encountered a tragedy that prompted the question, Why? *Why is there suffering in the world that seems so unfair?*

Assorted answers have been given, their sheer number a clue to the unsatisfactory nature of each. I want to look at the most common theories and offer you my thoughts. They are:

- God is teaching us a lesson.
- What looks bad now will turn out to be good.
- Human beings sin, and sin wreaks suffering.
- An evil deity (Satan) exists.
- Human beings make mistakes that result in accidents.
- Natural laws and processes of the universe can cause tragedies.
- God created the world but is no longer directly involved in what happens.
- Suffering is a mystery.

God Is Teaching Us a Lesson

Some people believe that God allows or inflicts suffering as a way of teaching us. They claim that God causes suffering in our lives to teach us some valuable lesson that will help us to live our lives more fully. Since it often takes something painful to jolt us out of complacency, God instructs us by striking us deeply.

An excellent portrayal of this way of thinking is found in the motion picture *Shadowlands*, in which Anthony Hopkins plays the popular British writer C. S. Lewis. Lewis was a Christian who believed that the greatest threat to one's belief in God is the problem of suffering. In the movie, Lewis says, "Pain is God's megaphone to awaken a sleeping world." He likens God to a sculptor who strikes us with a chisel again and again, causing pain because there is no other way for us to become the work of beauty that God intends.

The movie stops short of reporting to us the crisis of faith Lewis actually experienced following the death of his young wife. In later writings, Lewis said he believed that his wife had to die in order for him to realize how inadequate his faith had been when his life was full of cheer and optimism.

Is that the God in whom we believe? A God who strikes down a young woman in the prime of her life for the purpose of teaching her husband that his faith is inadequate? And what of her two young sons? Born during her former marriage to an alcoholic, the boys had already experienced trauma. What was God's "instruction" to them? Do we believe that God sends people brain tumors and allows planes to drop from the sky in order to teach us lessons? That might help to make the world seem orderly and under God's control, but it so offends our sense of what is right and fair and just that most thinking people cannot accept that God would act this way. Surely God could achieve the same results through less destructive means.

What Looks Bad Now Will Turn Out to Be Good

The idea that God inflicts suffering in order to teach us a lesson is related to another theory: What looks bad now will turn out to be good. Suffering may appear to be tragic and unjustified, but eventually it leads to something better. If we could see into the future, we would realize that suffering will bring about a greater good.

This idea was offered to me one Sunday morning following a worship service in which I had preached a sermon on unjust suffering. A young woman from our congregation asked, "Doesn't suffering bring strength to our lives?" It was a good question from a sincere person wanting to affirm suffering's positive side. And what she said was true—occasionally. Suffering can make a person stronger. I have experienced it in my own life, and over the course of my ministry I have witnessed it many times in the lives of others.

But not always. Some people are strengthened by suffering, and others are broken. I have known people whose lives were shattered by the death of their child. First they lost their religious faith because they had believed that God would not allow such a tragedy to occur to them, and then their marriage fell apart. They could not move beyond their bitterness and anger.

Perhaps you remember this tragic story reported in the media a few years ago. Three men had gone deer hunting for the day—a father and son, and a good friend of the father. At some point during the day, the father took aim at what he believed to be a deer and squeezed off a shot. When he reached the site of his target, he could not believe what he had done. The father had shot and killed his son. The pain was more than he could bear. He turned his gun on himself, doubling the grief and suffering of his wife.

If God is using a present tragedy to usher in some greater good, the father who shot his son to death certainly didn't know it. And why doesn't God accomplish the goal with less devastation? In fact, if God can do anything God wants, why must there be any innocent suffering to bring about a greater good?

Why do some people hold on to the belief that God always has a reason for such things? The answer has to do with control. Most people believe that nothing happens in the world that is beyond God's control. They believe that either (1) God caused it or (2) God could have prevented it. It follows that if God is in control, then anything that occurs must happen for a reason. That is, it must be part of the divine intention. This is a notion I will challenge in this book.

Many people imagine God to be like a wonderful human father, except on a much grander scale. They imagine a Super-Father who can do whatever He wants. Further, they suppose that one of God's primary tasks is to protect us and to keep us from harm. This idea is comforting until we are struck by a profound crisis and innocent suffering.

Human Beings Sin, and Sin Wreaks Suffering

Of course, not all suffering is innocent. A great deal of pain results from the fact that human beings sin. Remember the fiery inferno caused by the wildfires in southern California that swept through neighborhoods and woodlands, destroying everything they touched? At least one of the individuals who ignited the blazes said he did it for fun. And who will ever forget the tragic scenes of the Los Angeles riots in the spring of 1992? A mob mentality ruled as people went berserk, dragging innocent motorists from vehicles, smashing store windows, stealing whatever wasn't bolted down, setting fire to business establishments, and shooting into crowds indiscriminately. And what about a catastrophe that touched the lives of people throughout this country and around the world, the bombing of the federal building in Oklahoma City? More recently, our nation was stunned by the killings at Columbine High School in Littleton, Colorado.

Fires. Riots. Bombings. Killings. Yet none of these events, no matter how tragic, begins to match the violence caused by war, perhaps the chief example of sin's destructive nature. When people fail to view others as fellow children of God and to heed religious teachings to love their neighbors, the potential for suffering is unimaginable. In Bosnia, Kosovo, and Rwanda, where wars were fought in the 1990s, suffering abounded. Such euphemisms as "ethnic cleansing" emerged to justify despicable actions.

Suffering that results from human sin is probably the easiest to reconcile in our hearts and minds, but it still presents us with a problem. We cannot help but wonder, If God can do anything, surely a merciful God could see fit to reduce the amount of suffering a little. Some believe that sin exists in order that we may learn that God's way is best. That is, some believe that God *could* stop sinful human conduct, but doesn't.

But that idea offends our sense of justice. *Why would God allow innocents to suffer as the result of someone else's sin?* The fatal car crash that ended the life of Princess Diana resulted when an intoxicated driver was speeding in excess of one hundred miles per hour. Why did God allow the mistakes of the driver to take the lives of others? Or what of the disgruntled employee who marches into his workplace and begins shooting randomly at people? Couldn't God direct the path of the bullets away from innocent people? What about Susan Smith, the young mother in South Carolina who strapped her three-year-old son Michael and her fourteen-month-old son Alex into the backseat of her car and then rolled it into a lake, drowning them?

An Evil Deity (Satan) Exists

Before the rise of modern science, demons and evil spirits were thought to be the cause of human illness and other problems. In the Jewish tradition, the idea of an adversary of God (the Hebrew word *satan* means "adversary") is very old. For centuries the adversary was conceived as a member of God's heavenly court. However, by New Testament times this figure had been transformed into the god of evil who rivaled God Himself.

The idea of Satan was an attempt to remove the blame from God for the pain and suffering people experience in the world. However, the notion created far greater problems than it resolved. For instance, how did Satan originate? Did God create him? Why can't God prevent Satan from spreading pain and evil throughout the world? Is Satan more powerful than God? Can Satan cause great pain and suffering that God is incapable of preventing?

The idea that innocent suffering is the result of an evil deity is illogical unless we believe that Satan is more powerful than God or that God does not care about the suffering Satan creates. I cannot accept either of these notions.

Human Beings Make Mistakes That Result in Accidents

Do you remember the Amtrak train that derailed and plunged into the Alabama swamp, extinguishing forty-seven lives? The wreck was caused by human error. The pilot of a tugboat was pushing a barge up the Mobile River when he became lost. A thick blanket of fog disoriented him, and he mistakenly headed up the wrong channel. Soon the barge struck one of the supports of a bridge, weakening it so badly that the weight of the oncoming train was more than it could handle. As the train passed over, the bridge collapsed and several cars of the Sunset Limited tumbled into the mud and water below.

Two days following this disaster, the headline on the front page of our newspaper read: "God Put a Person There for Her." It was a statement by one of Andrea Chancey's school teachers. Andrea was a passenger in one of the cars that became submerged in the water. She was an eleven-year-old girl with cerebral palsy who was confined to a wheelchair. In the critical moments immediately following the crash, someone pushed Andrea out of a train window and into the murky water. Lillian Beech, a sixty-seven-year-old woman traveling in the same car, pulled Andrea from the water. Andrea's math teacher in Florida was quoted as saying, "I feel like God put a person there for her to hold on to."

At first glance, that is a lovely thought, but on further reflection, it makes me wonder. If God could put a person there to save the life of Andrea, *why couldn't God have prevented the wreck in the first place?* Both of Andrea's parents perished in the tragedy, along with forty-five others. When the pilot of the tugboat was lost and about to strike the bridge, why didn't God prevent the catastrophe by gently nudging the barge three feet to the left, allowing the barge to miss the bridge? Just three feet would have done it. Why does God allow such accidents to occur? Wouldn't God prevent them if God could?

At this point, we may not be able to understand why God *permits* such things (it will be clear later), but we can see that much grief is undoubtedly the result of human faults—ignorance, accidents, or sin. The more troubling notion is why suffering occurs from so-called natural disasters.

Natural Laws and Processes of the Universe Can Cause Tragedies

On December 26, 1996, a fierce winter storm hit the West, dumping huge amounts of snow in the mountains and record rainfalls in other parts of the region. As the first storm was beginning to dissipate, a second storm blanketed the area, and then a third. Rivers began flowing out of their banks, and levees began to break. California officials said it was the worst flooding in the state's history. More than 100,000 people were evacuated from their homes, mud slides buried roads and took out bridges, 2,000 people were stranded in Yosemite National Park, and 29 people lost their lives.

On May 3, 1999, killer tornadoes packing winds in excess of 300 miles per hour ravaged several communities in Oklahoma and Kansas, killing 48 people and injuring scores of others. In photographs the devastation resembled a bombing site, yet those who visited the area said that the actual destruction was much worse than any pictures could portray.

However, these terrible storms were dwarfed by the catastrophic hurricane that hit Central America in the fall of 1998. Hurricane Mitch, one of the worst storms of the twentieth century, dumped several feet of rain on four Central American countries, producing deadly floods and suffocating mud slides. Entire villages were obliterated without a trace. More than 9,000 people were known to have been killed by the storm, and several thousand more have not been accounted for. One million people were left homeless, over 100 bridges collapsed, and 70 percent of Honduras's crops were wiped out.

As is the case with most major catastrophes, it prompted many people to wonder, Why? *Why do such disasters occur?*

Until a few centuries ago, people offered explanations in terms of divine intentions. When a disaster occurred (what we call today a "natural disaster"), the question would not have been, Why did this happen? but rather, Why did God make this happen? And the answers were generally that God was punishing people for their sins, or God was warning people to change their ways (à la Sodom and Gomorrah). In Genesis, the epic flood was interpreted as God's method of wiping the slate clean of the widespread wickedness permeating the planet.

Today we interpret the suffering caused by natural disasters in terms of weather patterns, human negligence (failing to observe building codes), or ignorance (building on a flood plain). The rise of modern science (which began about 500 years ago) prompted this pivotal shift in human thinking. As modern science enabled us to understand the natural laws and processes of the universe, the idea that God wreaks havoc as divine punishment for sin was slowly pushed into the background. The biblical explanations of divine wrath, which had made sense to people for thousands of years, no longer rang true. In time they were discarded.

Does this mean that the Bible is unreliable? I don't think so. I believe it is essential to keep in mind that during biblical times people were extremely limited in their understanding of the world and its processes. Through no fault of their own, they did not know that the earth is one of nine planets in our solar system, and that these planets revolve around the sun. They possessed very primitive ideas of physics. They had absolutely no conception of gravity and could hardly have imagined that "up" for a person standing on the North Pole is the opposite direction for someone standing on the South Pole (or that poles even exist!). They had no clue that human beings had existed for tens of thousands of years, that plants had existed for millions of years, and that the age of the earth was in the billions. They had no notion that forms of life slowly evolve into more complex forms of life. They had no concept of bacteria or viruses. Their explanations fit with the best-known "science" of their day but no longer make sense now that we better understand the physical processes of the universe. What we must keep in mind is that their understandings (their primitive science) shaped their view of the world and how God interacted with it. Modern science has clearly demonstrated the inadequacy of this view.

The Scriptures were written in prescientific times when people possessed a *supernatural* view of the world. In the supernatural worldview, God exists "up in heaven" but occasionally *intervenes* in events here on earth by interrupting the normal flow of events. For example, in biblical times, people saw God's hand in preventing rain and interpreted the resulting famine as a sign that God was punishing people for wrongdoing.

Conversely, if things were going very well and the people were prospering, they interpreted the prosperity as a blessing from God. Modern science has totally changed our picture of the physical universe, and this has had a direct impact on our understanding of God's interaction with the world. God is no longer thought to send natural disasters or diseases as punishment. Rather, these things occur as a result of the same natural laws and processes of the universe that make our planet inhabitable. Thus, some of the same forces that produce a refreshing breeze can at times create a tornado. Some of the same processes that bring much needed rain to arid land at times create a hurricane. God doesn't whip up a hurricane (or earthquake or tornado or avalanche), and God doesn't create the bubonic plague (or cancer or AIDS). These things result from the natural processes that make life possible. Thus, we can state that some human suffering is caused by the natural laws and processes of the universe.

But that prompts a question: Why can't God prevent these natural processes from causing suffering? My answer to this question will become evident later, but many people believe the answer is found in God's retirement from the scene.

God Created the World but Is No Longer Directly Involved in What Happens

Sir Isaac Newton, who remained deeply religious, demonstrated that the world can be understood in mechanical terms. That is, the world operates on its own according to certain laws, and it does not need divine intervention to keep it going. It was not long before people used the analogy of a clock to think of the world, and God as the clock-maker who set it in motion. In the minds of many, God was distanced from the world, but not totally absent from the world. Whenever something occurred that did not fit with current theories, it was thought to be an intervention by God. However, with advances in science, fewer and fewer things were thought to be the result of divine intervention. God became more and more remote.

This led to a different conception of God, one that fit with our new understanding of the world and provided an explanation of why unjust suffering occurs. It is the idea that God created the world but is no longer directly involved in what happens.

Two hundred years ago, Thomas Jefferson wrote a book entitled *The Life and Morals of Jesus of Nazareth*. The book is actually an edited version of the Gospels. Jefferson removed those passages dealing with miracles and supernaturalist thinking (for example, Jesus walking on water) and constructed a more palatable version of the life of Jesus for those who held a scientific view of the world.

Less than a century later, Charles Darwin struck another monumental blow to the traditional view of God. His theory of evolution undermined the traditional interpretation of the creation stories in Genesis. As time went on, people began to come to terms with the evolutionary character of the world and thus felt further distanced from the Church and its supernaturalist thinking. The influence of such thinkers as Sigmund Freud and Karl Marx cast further doubt on the entire religious enterprise. Some people surrendered their Christian beliefs altogether. Their attitude can be captured in a comment made in 1878 by Max Müller, a distinguished anthropologist: "Every day, every week, every month, every quarter, the most widely read journals seem just now to vie with each other in telling us that the time for religion is past, that faith is a hallucination or an infantile disease, that the gods have at last been found out and exploded."[2]

Actually, what was "found out and exploded" was not belief in God. Rather, it was the previously held view of the world—supernaturalism. This is why some people have given up belief in God and others have become resigned to the idea that God set the world spinning in the beginning but no longer intervenes in the course of events. They contend that natural disasters can snatch away innocent lives because God is no longer directly involved in the ongoing events of our planet.

In the coming chapters, it will become obvious that I do not share this idea. I believe God is actively involved in the world. But if God is actively involved, then why is there such widespread suffering? Some have reached the conclusion that it is impossible to find a clear answer other than to say:

Suffering Is a Mystery

For some time now, a popular answer has been that some questions cannot be answered. Their solution is a mystery. That is, our finite nature, which comes with being human, prevents us from understanding why some things happen as they do. We cannot know all the ways of God. We cannot comprehend why a loving God, with the power to control events, would allow terrible things to happen to people. Our task is to learn to live with the mystery. We accept the paradox as part of our faith.

This answer speaks to many, but increasingly people are finding this reasoning more troubling than helpful. As the result of instant communication, more than ever before in the history of the world we are exposed to widespread suffering throughout our nation and throughout our planet. How can people of faith make sense of all the pain and suffering in the world?

I believe what is needed today is nothing less than a new way to understand God. But our new ideas cannot be based simply on someone's personal opinion. We must reinterpret traditional ideas about God by incorporating the contemporary view of the world. After all, traditional ideas about God were not shaped in a vacuum. They were influenced by the ancient (supernatural) view of the world. Now that the supernatural worldview has proven inadequate, some of the ideas about God created by the supernatural worldview are also inadequate.

When I use the phrase "contemporary view of the world," I am not referring to the cultural views of secularism, materialism, individualism, and the like. Instead, I mean that view of the world that has been influenced by the philosophical ideas of the physical sciences and is now widely accepted as the way the world functions. Specifically, these are the theories of evolution, indeterminism, and relativity. *Evolution* has taught us that nothing remains the same forever. Everything is changing and evolving. *Indeterminism* has helped us to understand that the future is open. Things are not destined to turn out one way and one way only. *Relativity* enables us to see that the world is not made up of separate and unrelated objects or events. Rather, the world is a web of interconnections. What happens in one place makes an impact on things in other places.

Whether or not we realize it, these three important theories account "for the developmental, dynamic, connectional, open way we think about things."[3] That is, they shape our view of the way things really are. For too long we have clung to an understanding of God that was shaped by the ancient view of the world. Now that our worldview has been revised, we must revise some of our ideas about God.

Do you remember *The Miracle Worker?* There is a beautiful moment in which Helen Keller discovers words. She realizes that words describe things. *Water* is the word for that cool wet thing running across her hands. It comes from something called a *pump*. And there are words for *mother* and *teacher* and everything she touches with her hands. Both deaf and blind, Helen Keller did not know that there were such things as words. But once she grasped the concept, she viewed everything in an entirely new light.

I believe it is essential for us to see God in a different light in order to be able (1) to understand why suffering exists, (2) to gain strength and healing from God, (3) to detect God's presence in our lives, and (4) to rediscover hope. I am driven by a firm belief that God is the

Creator of the world. Thus, what we learn about the world through science is in some ways a reflection of God and how God interacts with the world. Both the message of Scripture and the contemporary vision of reality must be taken into account on this journey, which will transform some of our notions about God. To this we now turn.

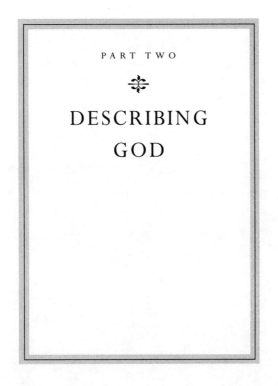

PART TWO

DESCRIBING
GOD

CHAPTER THREE

God Feels Every Ounce
of Our Pain

If you have suffered the loss of a loved one, you know how debilitating grief can be. Deep sadness can consume you and distract you to the point where you're able to accomplish very little. Simple everyday tasks that you had taken for granted become major ordeals. You search for help. You hunt for any advice or wisdom that will crack open the door enough to let a shred of light shine in to assist you in moving beyond your sorrow and the gnawing feeling of emptiness within.

There are practical things that often produce a measure of relief. You can throw yourself into your work or become engrossed in a project that not only occupies your time but stimulates your mind. Many people have found healing through writing their feelings in a daily journal. Some have even published books. Another means of finding relief is to force yourself out of the house, *away* from the television (which generally places you in a passive mode) and into the company of other people. You can search out a support group—or create one where none exists—of people who have suffered a similar loss. If you have children or grandchildren, you can become more involved in their lives and activities. You can involve yourself in helping others. (Countless volunteer opportunities exist.)

In addition, you can join a church, mosque, or synagogue whose leaders are sensitive to the deep pain caused by suffering. Within a religious community, our spiritual nature can receive nourishment. Logic and reason are wonderful attributes, but people are not objects. We are *subjects* whose lives take on meaning and purpose when we discover divine acceptance and hope. Life becomes not merely bearable but worth living when we possess a genuine hope that the pain will subside and some measure of joy will return to our lives. Religious faith can give rise to such hope.

All of these are important ways of moving forward with our lives. However, it is also extremely necessary to make sense of our suffering. Most of us cannot work through our grief adequately until we discover answers that seem reasonable to us. We do not find comfort or healing if our religious answers are at odds with our understanding of the world. Healing is likely to elude us if our concept of God makes no sense in light of our actual experience of suffering and evil.

What answer have you found most helpful to explain the existence of innocent or unjust suffering? I have found it necessary to think of God in a new light. A new world opened to me when I discovered an understanding of God that enables me to see the reason for innocent suffering and widespread evil.

A good place to begin our search for a new understanding of God is the Book of Job. In the opening verses of that book, we discover that Job was an exceptional person, blameless and upright. He was obedient to God, rejected evil, and was truly blessed. He had ten children (this was obviously at a time before people had to pay college tuition!), 7,000 sheep, 3,000 camels, 500 oxen, 500 donkeys, and a great number of servants. Job, we are told, "was the greatest of all the people of the east" (Job 1:1–3).

Then one day, his life came crashing down around him. Messengers came to him to say that all of his oxen, donkeys, and camels had been stolen and all of the servants watching them had been killed. Lightning struck and killed all of his sheep and the servants who were tending them. As Job was reeling from the tragic news, another messenger entered and gave him the most devastating message of all: All of his children, who had been feasting together under one roof, were crushed when the house collapsed. Job was overcome with grief.

It wasn't long before three of Job's friends came to comfort him. After being with him for several days, the friends began to ask Job what he had done to deserve all of this. He must have been guilty of something, so they kept prodding him, trying to extract a confession. But Job had done nothing wrong. He was the greatest man in all the East. He was the least likely candidate for suffering in the old way of thinking. The writer wanted to be as clear as possible that suffering could come to the most righteous people. Suffering does not afflict only people who deserve it. Good people also suffer tragedies. How do we account for that?

Sometimes there is no reason beyond accidental circumstances. Some want to hang the blame on God, but God is a loving and merciful God who wants the best for us. God does not desire for us to suffer.

When tragedy strikes us personally, it can feel as if God has abandoned us. We experience anger and anguish and cannot understand why God let such a thing happen to us. These feelings are normal when we face a crisis of faith. If we have lulled ourselves into a false sense of security by telling ourselves that God will keep us safe from harm, we can be devastated when a catastrophe strikes.

A woman in my congregation shared with me the picture of God she held as a child. Her father was a reckless driver, and whenever he drove in the mountainous area near their home, she would imagine God's hand on top of their car guiding them to safety. As a child, this concept enabled her to combat her fear. But as she grew older and witnessed profound suffering—including fatal car accidents involving children—this idea became increasingly difficult to maintain.

Where did we ever get the idea that God will protect us from pain and tragedy? Some will say this notion comes from the Scriptures, but the Bible also tells us of those who received no such protection. In addition to Job, consider what happened to some of the most faithful followers of God we find in the New Testament. Begin with Paul, the first great missionary to spread the Christian gospel. He was imprisoned, whipped with the thirty-nine lashes five different times, beaten with rods by the Romans on three separate occasions, and shipwrecked and left adrift at sea. There were times when he had no food and no shelter. Once he was nearly stoned to death. And then his life apparently ended after being imprisoned in Rome.

Or what of the great disciple Peter, a leader of the early church? He died by being crucified upside down. And what about John the Baptist? He was the cousin of Jesus, and the messenger of God who was to prepare the way for the coming of Christ. While Jesus was still alive, and only a few miles away, John the Baptist rotted away in prison until he was finally beheaded. And of course,

God's own son was crucified. How can we dare to think that God is going to keep *us* from harm when these great figures endured such terrible suffering?

God does not make pain and suffering disappear from our world. That is obvious, not only from the events of history but from reading each day's newspaper. Does that mean that God is not involved in the events of the world, or that God possesses little real power? I don't think so. In constructing a new image of God, we begin with how God responds to human suffering. I believe God *lightens the burden of human suffering by feeling our pain and taking some of the pain upon God's self*. In fact, I would say God is nearest when we suffer, and God's presence gives us strength.

To some, this sounds like a radical notion because the orthodox tradition has often denied that God is affected by what goes on in the world. The thinking has been that if people or events affect the Creator, then a change takes place in God. That is, God becomes vulnerable. And to some, vulnerability is weakness. It suggests that God is less than perfect.

But throughout the Bible we are told that God is affected by what happens. For instance, the prophet Hosea informs us that God feels great pain as a result of the unfaithfulness of Israel. We read, "How can I give you up, O Ephraim. . . . My heart recoils within me, my compassion grows warm and tender" (Hosea 11:8).

Numerous passages in the Old Testament provide examples of God becoming distressed and angry at the people of Israel for their unfaithfulness.

In the New Testament, Jesus expresses the righteous indignation of God through words and actions in episodes such as the expulsion of the money-changers from the Temple. In the parable of the wicked tenant, God is pictured as outraged at the rejection of his son (Matthew 21:33–41), and in the parable of the prodigal son, the father (who represents God) is overjoyed at the return of his wayward son (Luke 15:11–32).

Moreover, at the heart of the Christian faith is the belief that Jesus is the special revelation of God. And what we observe in Jesus is not an almighty Super-Father who is unaffected by events in the world. Instead, we encounter a *suffering servant*. Jesus was arrested, handed over to the Roman authorities, and crucified on a cross. He did not demonstrate his power by coming down from the cross and defeating the dark powers that sought to kill him. Instead, he demonstrated his power through his love for the world. He refused to stop loving even the very ones who were killing him ("Father, forgive them, they do not know what they are doing"), and his love was unconquered even by death. In Jesus, God feels the intense pain of innocent suffering. Thus, God would never wish such suffering on us. Instead of wishing it on us, God identifies with it. When we suffer, God suffers. When we experience pain, God experiences pain. The Creator affects the creation, and the creation affects the Creator.

Christian tradition has described God as the *unmoved Mover* and the *wholly Other*. But is it such an awful thing to think that God grieves when we suffer? Isn't One who is present with us in our suffering more helpful than One who stands at a distance? In fact, isn't God's presence with us in suffering the very *source* of our healing?

Several years ago the twenty-four-year-old son of a prominent Protestant minister was driving late at night when he lost control of his car. He skidded off a bridge and plunged into Boston Harbor, where he perished. After the son's death, his father preached a very moving sermon refuting the notion that the accident had been the will of God. Instead, he said, as the waves enveloped his son's sinking car, God's heart was the first to break.[4]

Suffering is very real. Suffering is extremely painful. However, we are *not alone* in our suffering. God feels every ounce of our pain and is present with us always, never abandoning or forgetting us. Our divine Parent alleviates some of the pain we experience by sharing our burdens.

It is comforting to know that God bears some of the weight of our suffering. But, if God does not wish us to suffer, then why does God allow it to happen in the first place? Is God in control of the course of events or not?

⁜

An Open Future

or

God Knows All Possible Futures

Not long ago in our community, an ambulance crashed into a van, claiming the lives of the twenty-eight-year-old babysitter who was driving and a beautiful three-year-old girl who was a passenger. The mother of the child was stunned when she was notified of the accident. She was already acutely aware of how a car wreck could change her life, because when she was eighteen she had been involved in a very serious accident that left her paralyzed from the waist down.

I do not know what friends said to this young mother grieving the death of her child, but I would not be surprised to learn that at least one person claimed the accident was God's will. Well-meaning people often make this comment in response to a tragedy. But is that what we are supposed to believe? That God had a purpose for taking these two lives?

How often have you heard people say, "When your time's up, it's up"? Many people believe that there is a designated day for their departure from earth, and that there is nothing anyone can do to change it. Such a belief stems from the idea that God is in control of everything that takes place in the world. In the sixteenth century, the Protestant reformer John Calvin helped give credence to this idea. Calvin wrote that "not a drop of rain falls but at the express command of God."[5] Calvin was resurrecting Augustine's fifth-century teaching that God is all-powerful and all-knowing. In doing so, he concluded that everything was firmly under God's control. According to Calvin, everything that happens in the world is a part of God's plan. He wrote that God is "the ruler and governor of all things, who in accordance with his wisdom has from the farthest limit of eternity decreed what he was going to do, and now by his might carries out what he has decreed."[6]

Calvin had *some* scriptural support for his ideas. For instance, in Psalm 135 we read, "Whatever the Lord pleases he does, in heaven and on earth, in the seas and all deeps. He it is who makes the clouds rise at the end of the earth, who makes lightnings for the rain and brings forth the wind from his storehouses."

The Westminster Confession, a statement of faith written in England approximately one hundred years after Calvin's life, continued Calvin's theology and was considered a standard for Presbyterians until recent times. The beginning of the third chapter reads: "God from all eternity did by the most wise and holy counsel of his own will, freely and unchangeably ordain whatsoever comes to pass." And in seeking scriptural support for this view, the writers of the document cite a verse from the Letter to the Ephesians: ". . . having been destined according to the purpose of God who accomplishes all things according to the counsel of his will" (1:11). John Calvin was especially fond of the writings of the Apostle Paul, who (at times) supported the notion that God strictly determines what happens. One of Calvin's favorite verses is found in Paul's Letter to the Romans: "So then [God] has mercy on whomever he chooses, and he hardens the heart of whomever he chooses" (9:18). Thus, it is no wonder that many Christians believe that tragedy reflects God's will.

If we strictly followed these passages and Calvin's theology, we would be forced to conclude that God's hand was involved in the recent car accident in our community (and every calamity). We would assume that God had a reason for what happened, and it would be perfectly correct to say that it was God's will. To some, that is comforting, because it means that everything happens for a reason. But on deeper reflection, this idea becomes very troubling. For one thing, it means that we have no freedom to make choices.

If God has predetermined all that is going to happen, then why live responsibly? If God has already predetermined the day I'll die (and everything that will happen in between), then it makes no difference how I live. I can drive my car in a careless fashion because my day has already been set, and nothing I do will either hasten the day or delay it. If God has predetermined what is going to happen, then what I do doesn't matter. I could become a drug dealer rather than a pastor and blame whatever happens on God. If God has predetermined what is going to happen, then nothing can be required of me. Such an attitude leads not to faith but to apathy, and eventually to despair.

But how we live *does* matter. And we *do* have choices. In the Book of Deuteronomy, God acknowledges this: "I have set before you life and death, blessings and curses. Choose life so that you and your descendants may live" (30:19). In the Book of Exodus, God says to Moses atop Mount Sinai, "Go down at once! Your people, whom you brought up out of the land of Egypt, have acted perversely; they have been quick to turn aside from the way that I commanded them" (32:7). The clear implication is that God wants the people to live one way, but they have rejected it and chosen another way.

When we read the New Testament, it is apparent that Jesus did not believe that God has predetermined all events. Otherwise, Jesus would never have spent so much of his ministry stressing the importance of how we decide to live our lives. Jesus encouraged his followers to be loving and forgiving. He explained to them the futility of trusting in wealth and material possessions. He told numerous parables, and the point of many of them was to inform people that there is a right way to live and a wrong way to live, and he fervently hoped they would choose the right way. His teachings are meaningless if people do not have the free will to decide what they will do.

There is another problem with believing that God has a purpose for everything that happens. It makes God responsible for the tremendous amount of violence, injustice, and suffering experienced every day by people around the world. Most people find that idea repulsive and incompatible with our notion of a loving God.

As I write, a critical Middle East summit has recently concluded, but no one knows if this has set the stage for a breakthrough for peace or for a further breakdown in relations. The political situation in Russia has yet to stabilize, and it appears that the Chinese government has stolen secrets from the United States that are enabling Chinese scientists to build sophisticated nuclear weapons. Communities across America are struggling to stem the school and community violence that marks our society. As you read this, there are undoubtedly other major concerns in the headlines. If someone said, "Don't worry, God has each of these things under tight control and is working them out as He has planned," would you be reassured? I wouldn't. To say such a thing would be to imply that God planned ongoing death and animosity in the Middle East, that God is toying with the people of Russia, and that God sanctions young people gunning down one another and occasionally allowing a stray bullet to end the life of an innocent bystander.

There is a part of us that wants to believe that God is in total control and won't let bad things happen to us, but there is also a part of us that would be repulsed by the thought that God is responsible for all the problems and the suffering in our world.

And how could any of us be held responsible for anything we do if God moves us around like pawns on a game board, maintaining strict control over the events of the world? We couldn't. Perhaps this is one of the chief reasons many of us cling to the idea. We do not want to be held accountable for our actions. We want an excuse.

So then, I offer a second observation about God: I believe God is the supreme power in the universe who is continually at work seeking to persuade the world toward greater forms of beauty and harmony, but *because we have freedom to make choices, God does not strictly control the events of the world*. When it comes to suffering, we can act courageously or cowardly. God will be there to feel our pain and share our burden.

Pastor Renee Ahern tells of watching a little girl in his congregation, named Amanda, who comes up for the children's sermon each week. She is a child of slight build, always in a beautiful dress, and always smiling. Amanda is fighting cancer. She has no hair, owing to chemotherapy, and her pale skin reveals the scars of her struggle. Yet she is a child with a smile. She has joys, and she giggles and often raises her hand eagerly to answer the minister's questions.

Amanda lives on the edge between life and death. She battles daily with the cancer that is ravaging her thin body and with the chemotherapy administered by the doctors who are striving to preserve her life. Even at the tender age of seven, Amanda knows of struggle and strength, of tragedy and triumph. There are no guarantees for Amanda. There are no immunizations against her suffering. There are no cures on the horizon. And yet Amanda is a very courageous little girl. Somehow she seems to know in the midst of her pain that God will not abandon her.[7]

Some people recognize that God cannot be in total control of the events of the world without being responsible for pain and suffering, so they suggest a modified view. They believe that God determines the outcome of *some* events, but not all. They imagine that God has set some boundaries, and only within those boundaries do we have freedom to make decisions. Doesn't that square with some things we know about life? Don't we recognize a number of things about ourselves that have been determined by something other than our own free will? Part of who we are has been determined by such things as where we grew up, what was going on in the world, our family situation, our physical health, our particular opportunities. Some things beyond our control have shaped us. Nevertheless, there are many situations every day of our lives in which we are free to make choices. However, if we say that we are free within certain boundaries while God still determines the outcome of some events, what do we mean? Which ones does God determine? And why wouldn't God determine that ambulances will not collide with vans filled with children?

I have found a different understanding that makes sense to me, so I offer my third and fourth observations about God. The third one leads directly from my second point, which is that God does not control events in the world because we have freedom to make choices. *God knows all the* possibilities *that might occur, but not even God knows exactly what will happen until it does.* That is, God's wisdom and knowledge are so vast that God comprehends all possible futures, but because we possess genuine freedom to choose, it is not possible for God to know precisely what will occur.

For instance, when the Allied troops landed on the beaches of Normandy in World War II, God did not know who would die and who would survive. That's because God did not direct the path that each soldier or bullet took. Those running onto the beach had the choice to run in a straight line, to zigzag, to crawl, or whatever. Those firing at them chose where to aim and shoot. If God had known on June 5, 1945, who would be killed the next day, then those running and those firing would not have had the freedom to choose their actions. What God knew the previous day *would have had to occur*, thus depriving them of their freedom on June 6.

At this moment, you have the choice to continue reading the next few pages of this book or to set it down and fix yourself a snack. No one, not even God, knows what you will decide to do. If God knew yesterday that today you will set the book down and fix a snack, then you do not currently have the freedom to choose what you will do. You *must* choose to fix a snack.

I believe that we are continually faced with choices. In each situation, God knows all the possible ways we might respond. Because God is affected by what goes on in the world and cares deeply for us, God wants us to respond in the best possible manner. So God encourages us to choose that which is best. This leads to my fourth observation: *Rather than coercing us, God persuades us toward our best choice*.

Improving our ability to discern God's desires for us will be discussed in depth in chapter 8. For now, it is critical for us to understand that the future has not been set in stone. We are free to make choices. *But freedom comes with a very high price.* Since God does not determine the outcome of events, vans loaded with children will continue to have accidents, people will get cancer, and wars will claim innocent lives. But how else could it be? If there is truly freedom and creativity in the universe, there must be both good and bad. If the decisions we make are to have any significance, there must be the possibility of pain and suffering. That said, I believe life remains hopeful because God seeks to persuade us toward the best possibilities. Our hope is in God's wisdom, which seeks to guide us in the best way possible.

Professor Tom Long tells of an occasion when he went grocery shopping. To put it mildly, grocery shopping is not Dr. Long's idea of a good time. On this particular occasion, he was already in a foul mood when he entered the store. He said his poor disposition deepened as he headed down the first aisle because there he

ran into a couple of people who were actually enjoying grocery shopping. It was a mother and her young son, and they had learned how to make a game out of grocery shopping. She would read him the first item on her list—paper towels, aluminum foil, whatever—he would hear what she said, and race around the store until he found what she needed, and then he would bring his trophy back to her shopping cart, place it in the cart, she would applaud him for what he had done, give him another item, and off he would go. They were laughing and having a great time with it all. Well, you know how it is when you meet somebody going down a grocery store aisle—you're going to meet them several times before you finish your shopping. It was about the third aisle over when it dawned on me that the little boy had a mental disability. The mother caught me staring at them. I said, "I was just admiring your relationship with your son." "Yes," she responded, "he is a gift from God."[8]

The woman could have blamed God for her child being mentally handicapped. She could have bargained with God, saying, "I will go to church every Sunday, and I'll help the needy if you'll heal him." But the woman must have realized that such a thing was not going to happen, and so she responded to the best possibility God presented her—to love, honor, and care for her son.

Since the future is open, tragedies will occur. One of the things that makes them bearable is how we respond to God's possibilities for us.

But how can we determine the best ways to respond? Does God provide us with any assistance?

✣

Persuasive Power

During the summer of 1990, our daughter Grandison served as a "Youth in Mission" in South America. The members of our congregation helped raise funds to make her dream trip a reality. Three days after graduating from high school, Grandison boarded a jet at Washington National Airport and flew off to Talca, Chile, where she was a guest in the home of the Reverend Luis Alberto and Nancy Merino, a Chilean minister and his wife who operated a school for mentally disabled children.

Grandison had never witnessed such widespread poverty, and after working at the school for one month she wrote us the following letter:

> Nancy and I just finished a long talk. At first we were simply talking about dogs, and I told her about sweet Lamb [our dog]. On Friday, one of my favorite little boys, Domingo, told me he had ten

dogs at his house. I mentioned that to Nancy in conversation. She looked at me very seriously and explained why. They love dogs, so they take in stray ones. That's one reason they take them in.

When Domingo first came to this school, his hand was cut up. Luz (the teacher in my morning class) asked him what happened. He said his dog bit him when they were killing it. Luz asked why they killed it, and he said, 'To eat it, why do you think?' He and his father had to kill their dog in order to eat! . . .

I just wonder—why does this happen? How could God let this happen? And who chooses who gets food and who doesn't? I wonder why some sweet loving people don't have much, and some jerks seem to have it all. . . . It's all so sad because it's not just Domingo—there are millions here like him.

After I return home, if I get upset because I don't have something, please remind me of Domingo.

Like so many others living today, Grandison was deeply troubled by the question, Why is the world so unfair? Behind this general question are more specific questions, such as, Why do hundreds of millions of people live in abject poverty? Why is there so much evil in the world? Why do innocent people suffer? These are the most difficult and demanding questions facing anyone who believes in God. In its simplest form, here's the problem:

1. God is loving.
2. God is all-powerful.
3. Evil exists.

You can choose any two of the three, and they make perfect sense. But once you affirm all three, a contradiction enters the equation. If God is all-powerful and loving, then evil should not exist. Yet evil *does* exist. And not just a little evil here and there, but widespread evil that causes tremendous suffering throughout the planet.

I believe that we can affirm the first and third points, but that we must come to a new understanding of the second. I believe that God is the supreme power of the universe who creates life and works to transform chaos into order and evil into good. However, I also believe that there are some things that God cannot do. If a mountain climber loses his grip and falls off a cliff, God cannot suddenly change the laws of gravity so that the climber will float softly to earth. If a driver falls asleep at the wheel and veers into a lane of oncoming traffic, God cannot grab the wheel and steer the car back into the proper lane.

This is a troubling notion to most of us when we first encounter it. A woman in my congregation spoke for many when she stated that she was very disturbed with the idea that there is something that God cannot do. She said she could believe that God *gives up* power by allowing there to be freedom, but she could not accept the idea that freedom simply exists in the universe, and God cannot change that fact.

It is essential for us to realize that we face a dilemma *either way* we think of God's power. If we say that freedom is simply a condition of existence and God cannot change that fact, we are troubled to think that there is something God cannot do. However, I find it even more troubling to believe that God gave up power to allow freedom to exist in the world. Because if God grants freedom, then God can take it away. If this is the case, then why doesn't God set minor limitations on freedom from time to time in order to prevent dire suffering? Surely there would be no great restriction of our freedom if God did not allow infants to perish in their cribs from SIDS or if God prevented stray bullets from killing innocent bystanders.

Most of us were taught that God can do whatever God desires. The retired seminary professor Dr. Burton Cooper has pointed out that this idea has come to function as a *given* in our definition of God. That is, the belief that God's power knows no limits has become so much a part of our understanding of God that it has become an *unquestioned premise* of our definition of God. It is time to look again at this premise.

I believe that we have misunderstood the *type* of power God possesses. Most people have accepted as a given the idea that the mightiest power that exists is the power to control and compel and coerce. If this type of power—let's call it "all-controlling"—is ultimate, then surely this is the type of power God holds. But is all-controlling power the supreme power? The power to compel is certainly impressive power. It gets its way and makes things happen. However, I believe it is not perfect power. I find it more helpful to think of divine power as perfect power.

And what is perfect power? The power of *persuasion*. All-controlling power is not perfect power because it does not allow for freedom. Perfect power is persuasive power because it takes into account God's just and loving nature *plus* the freedom that exists in the universe. God's power is not the power of a ruthless dictator to compel or coerce, but rather the power of a loving parent who persuades, urges, attracts, and coaxes. "The biblical image is of one who stands at the door and knocks, but who never forces entry."[9] I believe God is our loving parent who wants the best for us and who urges us to move in the best possible direction. God is not a dictator who compels us to act according to divine commands.

Don't all of us know good people who have prayed that their loved ones would not suffer and die, yet their loved ones did experience pain and die? Hospitals are filled with people praying for health, and war-torn countries are filled with people praying for peace, but the dying continues. What is the problem? Is God unaware of the grief and suffering? Or is the problem that God does not possess the coercive power to redirect events?

If you have ever prayed for a loved one not to die, you may have experienced extreme disappointment with God. It sometimes comes as a shock to people to discover that the Bible gives voice to such frustration. The Old Testament prophet Habakkuk writes, "O Lord, how long shall I cry for help, and you will not listen? Or cry to you 'Violence!' and you will not save?" (1:2).

Early in 1995 a young woman in my congregation named Erica, only twenty-one years old, died very suddenly. She was in her final semester of college, doing her student teaching, when she was struck with a pulmonary embolism. Her parents had spoken with her by telephone the previous night and were glad to discover that Erica was recovering from a bout with the flu and looking forward to being with her class of kindergartners the following day. The next morning, shortly before sunrise, Erica's roommate was awakened by the sound of her falling to the floor. Her roommate leaped out of bed and turned on the light to find Erica lying on the floor, already dead.

As you can imagine, members of our congregation were stunned, and her parents were devastated. She was their only child and, as her mother said to me a few hours after hearing the news, "our only hope for grandchildren." Now, at the young age of twenty-one, on the verge of becoming a kindergarten teacher, she was gone. The joy of their life, the center of their love and affection, was gone. Surely we can admit that there would be no great restriction of our freedom if God had intervened and not allowed a pulmonary embolism to take the life of this fine young woman.

How will Erica's parents survive this tragedy? Where will they find the strength to go on living? They will not find it in the glib suggestion that God must have taken Erica because God needed someone to work with the children in heaven. And heaven help the person who says, "You just have to accept it, it's God's will." *It is not God's will for children to die*.

- Perhaps they will find comfort in the belief that *unjust suffering is not God's will*. God is our loving parent who desires good things for us. It is not God's will that we suffer.
- Perhaps they will take heart in the idea that *God is affected by our suffering*. Since God is not detached from the world, God grieves when we suffer. When we

hurt, God hurts. God is with us in our pain. As the Apostle Paul says in his Letter to the Romans, "Nothing in all creation will be able to separate us from the love of God."

- Perhaps they will gain understanding in the notion that *God does not have strict control over everything that happens*. God knows everything that *can* happen in the future, but since freedom exists, God cannot compel circumstances as we might desire.

When we are young, we believe that our parents can do anything. They love us and care for us and provide everything we need. But as we grow older, there comes a time when we begin to doubt their power. There is also a time when we become aware that although they are able to shelter us from much harm and destruction, they cannot protect us from the inevitable pain and threats to our lives that come from living. Of course we maintain faith in our parents even though they cannot keep us from all harm. Could it be that we might find it necessary to make a similar progression in our religious faith in order to make sense of our lives?

✣

CHAPTER SIX

"I'm Praying for a Sweet Potato"

God is the supreme power in the universe—nothing even begins to approach the power of God—yet God does not possess unlimited power. God does not have a monopoly on all power but instead creates beings who have the power that comes with the freedom to make choices. If we genuinely experience freedom, then God's power is limited to some extent.

If God's power does not determine everything that happens, what does God's power do? Some seem to think that if God cannot do everything, then God is a weakling. I disagree. We would never say, "If the professor cannot answer every question, he is a useless professor." Or, "If the physician cannot diagnose every illness, she is a worthless physician." Such statements are nonsense. Indeed, the professor may open wonderful new worlds to us through brilliant insights, and the physician may save numerous lives through her expertise. Admittedly, these are crude analogies, but I trust they make the point.

I believe God works tirelessly to draw the world toward greater forms of order and harmony, without which there would be chaos and life would not be sustainable. God "is the ordering principle at the heart of the universe."[10]

The Bible begins with these words: "In the beginning God created the heavens and the earth." Some take that to mean that there was a moment, in the distant past, when God created our world. Past tense. God created, and that is why it now exists. However, the Hebrew words cannot be translated that precisely. In fact, the words can also be translated, "When God *began* to create . . ." This second translation carries with it the notion that God has not stopped creating but is continually creating. In addition, the passage goes on to say that the earth was formless and chaotic and covered in darkness.

This idea fits very well with our current understanding of the universe as a continuously changing cosmos. I believe God continues to work with the chaos, drawing the world to higher degrees of order. Rabbi Harold Kushner reminds us that as a result of this process we have certain laws of nature, such as gravity and chemistry and the other physical processes that make life possible. These laws of nature are reliable. If they were not, life would be filled with turmoil. For instance, if you hold a brick out in front of you and drop it, it will fall. That works 100 percent of the time. Gravity makes the world predictable in certain ways. We can construct buildings with the assurance that the materials will not begin to float away. We can leave the car in the driveway without fearing that it will drift off into space. But gravity also causes problems. Sometimes when things fall, they strike people. If an airplane loses its power, it plummets to the ground.

The air, the wind, and the rain make life possible, but sometimes they also combine to create tornadoes or hurricanes or floods. If this occurs where people or wildlife are present, there are casualties. I believe one reason for innocent suffering is that God has not written the final chapter on the creation story but is still at work creating order out of chaos. Thus, natural disasters can claim innocent lives.

Remember the opening story of the golf course with monkeys? To me, it is a metaphor for why some bad things happen. The monkeys represent those things that cause us grief and whose origin is unclear. God does not will for people to get cancer or to be wiped out by hurricanes, but since God does not maintain strict control over everything that happens and is still working to bring order out of chaos, terrible tragedies can strike our lives.

I believe that, in addition to bringing order and making life sustainable, God guides us. It is doubtful that, left entirely to ourselves, we humans would have gotten very far. We may be free to make decisions, but we do not always make wise ones. God guides us toward the realization of love and justice and beauty. Our hope turns to despair if our hope is only in ourselves. However, our hope is in God's wisdom, which seeks to lead us toward a world where "the wolf can lie down with the lamb" (Isaiah 11:6), where "swords shall be beaten into plowshares" (Isaiah 2:4), and where people will love God with all their hearts, minds, and souls and will love their neighbors as they love themselves (Mark 12: 29–31). The wisdom of God gives us a vision of a better world for which we can strive. (How God guides us will be discussed in chapter 8).

Along with guidance, God gives us strength. The death of a child or young person can be debilitating. The loss of any loved one can drain us of all energy and motivation, but God can provide us with the strength to put the pieces of our lives back together and to go on living. Many people have known times in their lives when they could not have persisted if they had not received strength from beyond themselves. In God we can find the courage and determination we need to survive difficulties and to move into the future.

In a church where I formerly preached, I have a friend named Richard who earns his living as a licensed clinical social worker. Richard is a bright and sensitive person, a man with a passion for fishing and hunting who used to keep himself in excellent physical shape by running several miles each day. I say "used to" because Richard was critically injured in a dreadful accident.

Attending an out-of-town seminar in March 1994, he rose very early in the morning to get in a vigorous run before his workshops began. Richard remembers walking outside to the parking lot and stretching before beginning his jog. He ran down the road for some distance before he was struck by a car. It was a gruesome accident. In addition to numerous internal injuries, one of his legs was severed. He was airlifted to a hospital in Louisville, where he spent two weeks in an intensive care unit. He was fortunate to survive.

My wife and I did not receive word of the accident for two months. When we called Richard to see how he was doing and to lend our emotional and spiritual support, he radiated a positive attitude toward his upcoming appointment to be fitted for his artificial leg and toward his physical rehabilitation program. But the central thing I remember from our conversation was this: Richard said, "I never would have made it through all of this without receiving strength from God."

God can give us the strength we need to persevere when the events of our lives threaten to crush us, when we feel we simply cannot go on. Or to be more precise, when we are *unaware* that God is with us. I do not believe God can make bad things simply disappear once they have happened. But through God's presence, we can discover the strength we desperately need to hang on until we realize that life still has meaning and purpose for us.

How does God strengthen us to endure? Richard had endless hours in which to think and to pray. Daily he prayed to God to help him accept what had happened and to give him the strength and determination to move forward with his life. There were setbacks and times of discouragement, but time and again God strengthened him. He told me, "I don't know how to explain it, except to say I had a *strong internal feeling* that God was with me and would get me through this." The strength did not come immediately, but rather gradually and incrementally.

When people experience an extremely difficult loss, there are generally moments when they feel worn out and ready to give up. Some people crumble at these critical turning points and never recover from their tragedy. Others find strength in God to persevere. They discover, through their conversations with God, that something critical happens: they begin to envision a new future, and along with it, they begin to sense the will to strive toward that future.

Jürgen Moltmann, one of the great German theologians of our time, grew up in a home where education and philosophy were extremely important but religious faith was not. When he was fifteen years old, he was pressed into military service by the Nazis. He was put in a uniform and given a gun in the final, dying days of the Third Reich. He said, "I was scared to death. And the first time I saw an enemy soldier I surrendered to him. I was walking through a forest in Belgium, and I ran into an Englishman, and the only thought in my mind was to get my gun down before he shot me and to surrender." He said, "I ended up spending four years in a prison camp—and it was the luckiest thing that ever happened to me."

Moltmann said, "An American chaplain came around giving out Bibles. And I was so lonely and hungry for something to read that I would have read anything." He said, "Do you know what part of the Bible comforted me most? It was the crucifixion of Christ. I was dirty and filthy and alone. I was serving a nation that had been crushed, and my world and the world of my parents was gone forever. But in a man dying on a cross, I discovered the strength I needed to make it through my troubles."[11] Moltmann began to envision a new future shaped by the undying love of God.

With the knowledge that God's love for us never ends, we gain confidence that we will not be crushed by the blows of life that threaten to destroy us. We discover strength because God will continue to work with our best interest in mind, shaping a new future for us.

In the summer of 1993, our local newspaper carried a story about a woman who hid for nearly a year with her five-year-old daughter. It all started back in 1986. The mother, named Mary, was leaving town on a business trip when her older daughter handed her a note. Mary put it in her pocket and decided to read it on the plane. She assumed that the note would say something along the lines of "I love you, Mommy. I'll miss you while you're gone."

But instead the letter read, "He molested me." Mary confirmed that the "he" was her husband, and she filed for a divorce. In less than a year her estranged husband was placed on probation by the courts when they found him guilty of fondling his eleven-year-old stepdaughter. Meanwhile, the couple's youngest child, who was four, told a baby-sitter that her father was molesting her when she visited with him. Mary began to fight to prevent unsupervised overnight visits with the father. The case dragged on, and Mary finally determined that the only way to protect her child was to go into hiding. She hid for nearly a year. Eventually the court ruled that the mother was justified in shielding her daughter from the visits and she was awarded sole custody. If that were the end of the story it would be somewhat happy. Tragically, it was not.

The mother died a short time after receiving custody. She died because shortly after going into hiding she discovered that she had cancer and she knew that if she sought treatment it would require identification and insurance forms and she would probably be discovered. And if she were discovered at that time, her ex-husband might be allowed unsupervised visits with their daughter. She decided that she would not subject her child to any more abuse. After the courts ruled in her favor, she came out of hiding and immediately went to her physician for treatments. But she had waited too long. The mother literally gave up her own life because of her deep love for her daughter.

I believe such intense devotion illustrates the kind of love that God has for each of us. God's love for us is a sacrificial love that never ends, not even with death.

A colleague has shared a memory of his father when he was a young boy. It was Christmas Eve, and his family of five was packed into the car on their way home from church after the Christmas Eve service. Bobby, age seven, was sitting in the backseat by the door of an old Nash Rambler made in the 1940s. In those models from the forties, the backdoor opened exactly opposite of the way car doors open today—right into the wind. As Bobby was sitting in the backseat, he kept staring at the door handle, wondering what would happen if he just flicked the handle. As you might imagine, Bobby's curiosity got the best of him, and he flipped that door handle. The wind caught it with a *whoosh*, and the door stood straight open toward the oncoming traffic. His dad hit the brakes and brought the car to a fast halt. As he did, Bobby dove for the floor. His mother turned to look at the backseat and, unable to see him, began screaming, "Where's Bobby? Where's Bobby?" His sister replied in a disgusted tone, "Oh, he's right here on the floor. He's all right." Bobby's dad stepped out of the car, leaned back against the hood, and took several deep breaths. Eventually he climbed back into the car, started it up, and drove the rest of the way home without saying a word. Bobby figured he was in *deep* trouble.

They finally reached home and pulled into the driveway, and Bobby was the first one out of the car. He sprinted into the house and stood next to the Christmas tree, hoping it would provide a measure of protection. His dad marched into the room and grabbed Bobby and gave him the biggest hug he'd ever given him. And he said, "Son, I'm sure glad you didn't fall out of the car. I'm sure glad you're still all right."[12]

In some ways, God is like that father. When we challenge the laws of physics, God cannot prevent car doors from flying open. But God is our loving parent whose concern for us never ends. God comforts us by sharing the burden of our pain, by enabling us to envision a new future, and by replenishing our strength when our own strength is exhausted.

Often the love, hope, and strength we need to keep going becomes evident through other people. That is because God inspires people to help others. I believe God cannot prevent accidents from taking innocent lives, but God inspires people to give love and support to ease the burden of those who suffer. God cannot prevent children from being born with birth defects, but God inspires people to go into research to find cures. The reason our daughter Grandison witnessed such dire poverty in Chile was because she was inspired to do whatever she could to help.

For most of my life, I did not recognize the importance of inspiration. Today I believe that life would be unbearable without it. Let me share a story.

On the morning of Thanksgiving 1995, National Public Radio's *Morning Edition* covered a story about a food bank in Lubbock, Texas. The food bank has been in existence for a number of years, and one of its primary goals has been to provide hungry people with fresh vegetables. This is often a formidable challenge. Sometimes the produce is simply not available. Other times there is such an enormous quantity that it spoils.

One fall day an eighty-three-year-old bedridden woman

named Alpha Campbell phoned the food bank with a special request. Alpha wanted a sweet potato. The executive director, Caroline Lenier, answered the telephone and had no choice but to disappoint the woman. She was sorry, but they didn't have one sweet potato in the whole place.

Undaunted, the elderly woman replied, "I'm praying for a sweet potato." And she added, "I'm praying for the food bank. And I'm praying for myself. And my daddy told me to eat a sweet potato every fall, but I haven't been able to afford one. So here's my telephone number." Lenier said she couldn't bear the thought of that gentle-sounding older woman praying to God for a sweet potato. Plus, she didn't want God to look bad, so she decided to make a quick trip to a grocery store to purchase a sweet potato for the woman.

However, when Lenier grabbed her keys and purse and headed out to the parking lot, she discovered that her car was blocked and she couldn't get out. A semitrailer had just pulled in, and the driver was climbing down from his cab. He walked to the rear of his forty-two-foot eighteen-wheeler and opened up the back. Lenier was astounded by what she saw: 42,000 pounds of sweet potatoes. The driver said, "They're too little to sell. They're ripe. They're ugly. That's why we got 'em. Nobody buys a little runty, ugly, sweet potato." Without saying a word, Lenier dashed back into the food bank.

She dialed Mrs. Campbell immediately and said, "Please stop praying. We've just received 42,000 pounds of sweet potatoes, and Mrs. Campbell, we don't have room for any more!" And Mrs. Campbell said, "I hope they're little ones. I just hate them big ones."

An amazing but true story. What do we make of it? How do we explain it? There was a time in my life when I would have considered such an event to be a supernatural miracle (God intervening in the natural flow of events). There was also a time when I would have said, "It was just a lucky coincidence." Today I see things differently.

I don't think it was a supernatural miracle, because I do not believe God works that way. I have been present with parents who have prayed their hearts out that their infant child would recover, yet the child perished. War-torn countries are filled with people praying for an end to the killing, but it continues nonstop, claiming innocent victims. The streets of our cities are filled with mentally ill people wandering the back alleys and living in their own private hells. Corrupt individuals get away with murder, steal millions, and live lives of relative ease. There is simply too much pain, too much suffering, and too much injustice in the world for me to believe that God can intervene whenever God wants and strike up a miracle. If that were true, then why would God be wasting time on truckloads of sweet potatoes when there are much more profound tragedies to mend?

On the other hand, I have a problem with the notion that the arrival of the sweet potato truck was no more than a fortunate coincidence. After all, why was that food bank in existence in the first place? Because people had been inspired to create such a place. I believe such inspiration comes from God. The human mind does not generate all thoughts on its own. In addition to self-creativity, we receive "impressions" and suggestions from outside sources. One of those sources is God. Our natural inclination is to look inward, to take care of ourselves. God inspires us to look beyond ourselves, to look to the needs of others. In a world without God, people would take care of only themselves and their loved ones. But in a world where God is actively involved, people are motivated to serve the poor and to feed the hungry, and they are motivated to do countless other things that they would not choose to do on their own.

Again, the central question revolves around our understanding of God's *power*. If the arrival of the sweet potatoes was a supernatural occurrence, then we believe that God uses power to force things to happen. That is, God not only created the conditions that would enable the sweet potatoes to grow but compelled a farmer to plant the sweet potatoes in the first place. And manipulated weather conditions to stunt their growth. And forced the farmer to forfeit his crop to the food bank, which God had manipulated people in Lubbock to create years ago. But is this the way life really works? Is God continually pulling our strings? Or do we have the freedom to make choices? Certainly we do. God desires that we act in particular ways, but God does not force us to act accordingly.

And yet I believe it would be a mistake to conclude that God is simply a neutral observer. God presents us with ideal possibilities, but we must ultimately decide what we will do with them. God deeply yearns for us to respond in the best possible way, but since people are genuinely free to choose, they often make choices that are less than ideal. I believe the arrival of the sweet potatoes illustrates how events can come together to produce a marvelous outcome when people embrace God's ideal possibilities.

Although God does not maintain strict control over all that happens in the world, it does not follow that God is a weakling. God is the most powerful force in the universe, bringing order out of chaos and making life possible. In addition, God is the source of wisdom, strength, and inspiration, all of which lead ultimately to hope and opportunities for new life.

CHAPTER SEVEN

The Power of Transformation

Larry Trapp, from Lincoln, Nebraska, was the Grand Dragon of the Ku Klux Klan and the head of Nebraska's American Nazi Party. Posters of his hero, Adolf Hitler, covered the walls of his dark, one-room apartment. He spent much of his time making threatening phone calls to blacks, Jews, and Asians who lived in Lincoln. Trapp was quoted as saying that he never harmed anyone physically, but he did admit to owning illegal weapons and ammunition. His declared reason for possessing them was to instill fear in others. "If you can do that," he said, "you feel like a big shot."

Michael and Julie Weiser settled in Lincoln believing it to be a nice community in which to raise their children. Julie still remembers the Sunday morning their telephone rang and Michael answered. It was the first of many contacts with Larry Trapp, who welcomed them to their new home with the following words: "You're going to be sorry you ever moved into Lincoln, Jew boy." Two days later, they received a package in the mail. A card on the top of the package read, "The KKK is watching you, scum."

This is one of the prices human beings must pay to live in a world where people are free to act in almost any manner they choose. Not only must we endure innocent suffering caused by accidents and the unruliness of nature, but we must also contend with suffering that is imposed on us by others. In our freedom, we can choose to live in ways that result in fairness and concern for others, or we can choose to inflict pain on others. Since God does not force his will on us, we are free to make countless decisions concerning how we will live our lives. Larry Trapp was obviously a mean-spirited person who enjoyed disrupting people's lives.

What help could God have been for the Weisers? They could hope and pray that God would strike Larry Trapp and all the rest of the KKK dead, but they knew that God does not act that way. The Weisers could not expect God to provide this sort of relief any more than prayers for the demise of Adolf Hitler or Saddam Hussein or Slobodan Milosevic prevented these leaders from destroying countless lives.

How could God help this Jewish family? For one thing, the Weisers could discover in God the strength to endure Larry's hatred. Through prayer, their belief in God's loving presence, and a vision (however sketchy) of a new and better future, the Weisers could find courage and determination to carry on in spite of the abuse they experienced. When they felt like giving up they could discover strength in a power beyond themselves that encouraged them to forge ahead in doing what was right—not returning hate for hate.

Another way God could provide help was by inspiring others. Some could be inspired to stand in solidarity with the Weisers, helping to ease their burden. Still others could be inspired to expose the individuals associated with the hate groups in Lincoln and perhaps undermine their power.

God was not indifferent to the pain experienced by the Weiser family. I believe God opposes suffering and evil because God is a God of love who desires good things for all people.

How can we make such a claim? It is not possible for us to make such a determination from our observation of the world or from our personal experiences. The evidence from these two sources is ambiguous. For instance, we may see beauty and order as we observe the radiance of the sun rising in the east, casting light onto the planet as it makes its way across the sky and casts gold as it melts in the western horizon. But what do we see when an earthquake violently rips apart the ground, destroying people and property? Or what of our personal experiences of life? If we live in a free country, have loving parents, and experience happiness, we may conclude that God is loving. But what would we conclude about God if we grew up in dire poverty with abusive parents and never experienced freedom?

Observations of the natural world and our personal experiences of life do not provide us with many clues about the nature of God. To make claims about the basic attributes of God we must rely on special revelations of God. Such revelations, found within the great religions of the world, become widely recognized as "truth" when they pass the test of multiple human experiences over time. One such revelation is that God is loving. Indeed, love is a concept that is revered in all the major religions of the world.

In addition, Jesus of Nazareth, recognized as a prophet by Muslims and some Jews (as well as by many Buddhists and Hindus—Mahatma Gandhi comes to mind) and considered the Son of God by Christians, revealed the nature of God through his life and teachings. Most enlightening in his revelation is the radical nature of the love of God.

Had Jesus lived a life of relative ease, his ceaseless love for others might serve as an impressive example. However, the fact that he continued to exude love when all he had worked for crumbled and he was crucified between two thieves serves as a powerful testimony of God's love. He even loved the very ones who were killing him, calling for their forgiveness with his dying breaths.

I believe the crucifixion is a powerful example of the boundless love of God. Neither intense pain nor death can destroy God's love. In addition, I believe Christ's resurrection demonstrates that God's love is the power of transformation that can lead to new life. This new life happens to us after we die (the subject of chapter 9), but is not limited to the occasion of our death. It is available every moment of our lives. God is constantly working to transform each person and each situation.

Let's return to the Weisers, who were being harassed by Larry Trapp. I believe that God felt the pain of that family, and that their suffering became God's suffering as well. God, then, sought to transform their situation by being present with them and by offering possibilities that might make their situation more tolerable—and might even transform Larry Trapp in a positive way. God seeks to transform us by persuading us to move in a new direction—the best possible direction given our circumstances. We still maintain the freedom to respond however we choose. We may accept or reject the urging of God. We may pursue the transformation that God desires to effect in our lives, or we may ignore it. (How we discern God's desires for us will be covered in the next chapter.)

Larry Trapp *could* be transformed into a better person, but not unless he embraced the possibilities that God presented to him. Keep in mind that Larry Trapp did not become a person of hatred overnight. When he was young, his father would gather Larry and his brothers and sisters in the car on Easter Sunday and say, "Let's go down to North Omaha and see how fancy the niggers are dressing today." Larry was also constantly subjected to derogatory comments about Jewish people. His father would often say to him, "Those Jews will try to screw you out of a dollar bill every chance they get. They're trying to take over the United States!"

Larry Trapp could not be transformed easily or quickly because his past had shaped him in many ways. In all of us, the past plays a significant role in who we become. Yet we still have the power to decide the manner in which our past will shape us. More important, the future has the power to alter our lives as we discern God's possibilities and live into that future.

Michael Weiser is a deeply religious man who is committed to his faith. One of the highest goals a human being can accomplish, he believes, is to change an enemy into a friend. Somewhere in the midst of the harassment he became determined to see whether he could change Larry Trapp from an enemy to a friend. Weiser began to call Trapp's apartment and leave friendly messages on his answering machine. After several calls, Trapp picked up the phone one day and angrily told Weiser to stop calling him. Weiser responded with kindness in his voice: "I know you are disabled. Would you like a ride to the grocery store?" After a minute of silence, Trapp said, "No, but thank you for asking," and hung up. Several weeks went by, and then one day Trapp called the Weisers and said he needed to talk. Michael responded that he and his wife would be right over.

That night Michael and Julie Weiser met with Larry Trapp for four hours. Trapp later said he never had met anyone who exuded such love and caring as this couple. He admitted to them that he was desperately lonely and unhappy with his life. Then he did something remarkable. He took two swastika rings from his fingers and handed them to the Weisers, saying he no longer wanted the rings. A friendship took root as Larry Trapp began to be transformed into a new person. But his transformation was not a one-night aberration in a life destined for darkness. He continued to shed his former existence as he responded positively to the best possibilities before him. It wasn't long before he had publicly apologized to both the Jewish and African American communities. Incredibly, he even converted to Judaism!

At some point, the Weisers discovered that Larry was in very poor health. Diabetes was slowly taking his life. The Weisers again responded with love, convincing him to move into their home.

Larry Trapp said he would try his hardest in the last months of his life to reach out to persons who were willing to rethink their racism. He said he would not simply preach at people: "Do this, don't do that." Instead, he invited others to see how much happier his life had become after he changed.

Julie Weiser eventually quit her job in order to take care of Larry full-time. A few months later, the former Ku Klux Klan Grand Dragon and leader of Nebraska's American Nazi Party died. Michael Weiser was cantor at the funeral. He sang not for a man who had died full of venom and hatred, but rather for someone who had been transformed into a man of love and peace.[13]

In this true story, we witness the transforming power of God at work. Larry Trapp responded positively to God's urging (most obviously through the Weiser family, but not solely through them) to reject his life of hatred and bigotry for a new life of love and justice. And although this may be difficult to fathom, God is similarly at work in every single person's life. At this very moment, God is seeking to persuade you to respond to the best possibilities before you. Are you open to the transforming power of God? Are your mind and heart genuinely open to the change God can work in your life?

I want to share with you something that occurred in my congregation. A few years ago, on the first day of

Sunday school, the teacher of our second-grade class welcomed all of her new students for the year. She was eager to become better acquainted with each one of them. That is, each one of them except for one particular little boy. She had heard about William from the kindergarten and first-grade teachers. To call him "a real handful" was something of an understatement. There had been problems in his home, and the boy seemed to be acting out his anger in the classroom. He constantly sought attention and often behaved in very destructive ways. He would interrupt the teacher repeatedly, get into scuffles with classmates, and often refuse to cooperate with an assignment. The teachers from the previous year had been as patient with him as possible, but they were greatly relieved to know he would not be returning to their classroom this year.

The second-grade teacher had been planning her strategy and preparing herself mentally throughout the summer. She had made up her mind to be very positive with him, to give him clear guidelines to follow, to keep him busy at all times, and constantly to let him know that she loved him and God loved him.

As she had anticipated, he pulled some of his favorite tricks. But as the weeks went by, the problems occurred with less frequency. William began to use his energy in constructive ways. A change was taking place within him. To be sure, the change was not rapid, but he was moving in the right direction. The teacher could see that his attitude and behavior were gradually improving.

Then one morning during our worship service it happened. As is the custom in our church, I invited all of the children to come to the front of the sanctuary for my children's sermon. I explained to them that each person in the world is a child of God, and to emphasize this point I took out a globe and placed it in the midst of them. Next I pulled out a piece of paper, folded it up, and began to clip it with scissors. (Knowing how clumsy I am with anything resembling a craft, most people were holding their breath to see if I could pull this off.) Fortunately, it worked, and when I stopped cutting and opened the paper, I had cut out several paper dolls that were connected, hand in hand. I stretched them out so they would encircle my globe. I explained that everyone on earth is part of the human family and it is important for us to respect one another and to help one another whenever possible. I was wrapping up my talk when William's hand shot into the air. I was thinking, "This has gone really well. The children seemed tuned in to the lesson. If I call on William, he may say something inappropriate and destroy the whole moment. Maybe I can act as though I don't notice his hand and quickly end my talk with a prayer." These thoughts raced through my mind in a split second. But I decided to take a chance and call on William, to let him know that I valued his comment. I looked his way and asked, "Yes, William, did you have something to add?"

"Look!" he exclaimed, pointing at the paper dolls and barely containing his excitement. "The way you cut them out made the shape of a heart between each person. It shows they love each other."

He was the only one who had seen it, but once said it was obvious to everyone. There was a heart of love between each of the dolls.

Was that the same child who had been so hateful and disruptive before? No, it wasn't. He had been transformed by love into a more caring and sensitive child. It did not happen overnight, and it took the combined efforts of many over a period of time. But that is how the transforming power of God often works in people's lives. It takes shape in small increments over time and is mediated through the words and actions of others. We just have to learn to detect it.

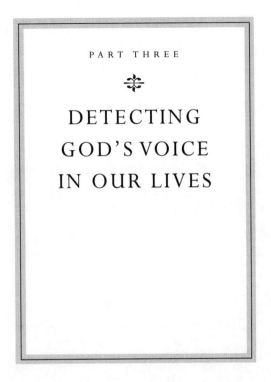

PART THREE

DETECTING
GOD'S VOICE
IN OUR LIVES

CHAPTER EIGHT

The Whispers of God

The profound changes in the lives of the former leader of the Ku Klux Klan in Nebraska and of young William are a radical display of the transforming power of God in a person's life. The question we must answer is, How can we become more alert to God's activity in *our* lives? Particularly when we are suffering?

I believe God loves us and yearns to bring healing to our lives. Since God does not force us to choose the best option available and we have the freedom to decide what we will do, we must choose to take part in the healing transformation. It is a bilateral effort. God persuades, urges, coaxes us in the direction of what is best for us. It is then up to us to accept or reject God's influence in our lives.

Although it has been several years, I remember hearing about the morning that forever changed Ellen's life. Without explanation, she was asked to leave her desk and to go to the personnel department at work. As she headed down the hall, she had an uneasy feeling, fearful of the news that awaited her. When she reached the office door and stepped inside, three people stood up quickly. One was her husband. Her mind raced forward. Why is he here? He doesn't leave work this time of day. What is he doing in this office? Something terrible has happened.

Her husband was on the verge of tears, and she felt her stomach creeping into her throat. Somehow she managed to ask what had happened, but even as she spoke, she knew she did not want to hear the answer. Her husband tried to talk, but all he could say was, "Robert." Their eighteen-year-old son Robert had been in a car wreck on the way to school. There were others in the car with him, and at first everyone seemed to have escaped the accident with a few scrapes and bruises. Robert had climbed out from behind the steering wheel, walked around to the front of the car to inspect the damage, and then, without warning, collapsed onto the pavement. Everyone rushed to his side, the rescue squad was called, and it arrived only minutes later, but there was nothing they could do. He was already dead.

Ellen's life was forever altered, and for a long time she did not believe the future offered anything. All she could see was the cruel snatching away of the hopes and dreams she had for her son. He had been such a positive young man and seemed destined for a career in a helping profession. Robert was a natural with children, and everyone knew that he would have improved the lives of countless others, but that could never become a reality now that he was dead.

For three years following Robert's death, Ellen's thoughts were dominated by what the future would *not* bring. She was engulfed by bitter feelings toward the other driver, toward God, and even though she knew it made no sense, toward the parents of the boys who had survived the wreck. Yet as intense as her bitter feelings were, they were often overshadowed by her profound sense of sorrow. She had never known that sadness and pain could pierce so deeply.

People who have encountered a tragedy know that during periods of intense grief, anger and despair not only dominate our waking hours but can also haunt us as we sleep. These deep feelings have the power to cloud our awareness of the fact that life is *not* over. Even though it may seem impossible, God still has rich possibilities for our lives. But two things in particular work against us. First, our anger and despair consume us so completely that we may come to believe that the present and the future have little to offer us other than continued grief and suffering. We hurt so intensely in the present that we may not honestly believe we can find relief from our sorrow in the days to come. This overwhelming pain causes us to miss many of the opportunities for healing that God places before us.

Second, we may unknowingly reject the possibilities that God presents us with because they appear so small in comparison to what we truly desire. The problem is that we yearn for what we cannot have. We want our loved one back. We want to wake up from this dreadful nightmare and have our lives back the way they used to be. But God cannot offer us this possibility—what has happened cannot be undone. God cannot suspend the laws of nature. Although Hollywood may tantalize us with scenes of going back in time and changing what has taken place, no such chance exists in real life. Instead, God presents us with the best possibilities *given our situation*. A grand, new, cheerful, and optimistic life is not immediately possible. The pain of our loss is not so quickly overcome; the intensity of our grief can be lessened, but only gradually. And so we must be alert to the small steps for improvement that will slowly lead us to a new life with a new future.

God seeks to heal us and to help us live rich and fulfilling lives. And God's way is to persuade us toward our best future. But how does God coax us toward what is best for us?

I believe God envisions all the possibilities for the future and presents us with the best opportunities for a rich and meaningful existence. How is it even possible to discern what God is inspiring and influencing us to do?

Our first task is to develop an attitude of expectation. We will miss what God is saying to us if we do not expect to hear anything. In fact, I believe we miss most of what God is saying to us because our hearts and minds are not anticipating God's influence in our lives.

God communicates with us in a variety of ways, including people, events, our intuitions, prayer, and Scripture. If we expect to glean a message from God, we must pay attention to what is going on in our lives and the variety of ways in which God may be seeking to influence us. We cannot simply charge ahead from one person and event to the next without ever reflecting on the possibility that God may be saying something to us through *this* person or *that* experience. It is likely that some person or some event has dropped a precious nugget in our laps and we missed it because we weren't expecting it. There is no telling how many priceless opportunities Larry Trapp overlooked before the Weisers finally made the difference. One can only guess how many good years he squandered because he allowed his past experiences rather than new opportunities to shape his thoughts and actions.

Keep in mind that people have detected the whispers of God in the most unlikely places. The Austrian composer Antonio Salieri heard them in the music of the irreverent and obnoxious Mozart. Imprisoned Jews detected it in the German businessman Oscar Schindler. The key is to develop an attitude of expectation in which we are always open to God's possibilities for our lives.

As we open up, we will begin to notice that there are numerous influences in our lives, including our friends and family. Each source carries its own degree of influence. Sometimes the influence is powerful; sometimes it is negligible. Most of the time we are not even conscious of the impact of these various influences.

Recently, in a conversation with a member of our congregation, I inquired how things were with her family. She responded, "Well, not that great. There's a very tense atmosphere in our house. My husband is under a lot of pressure at work, and it's really affecting his attitude. He doesn't horse around with our children or laugh much anymore. Everyone just tries to stay out of his way."

We often overlook the impact that others have on our lives. We may forget that we are constantly being influenced by numerous sources outside ourselves: the ideas and attitudes expressed by others, the items we read, the day's weather, the type of music we listen to, the temperament of our home or workplace, the worship services we attend, the meaningful conversations we have with others, the movies we watch, sporting events—and the list continues.

In addition to the many external influences, there are also internal influences. Modern psychology has made us aware of the persuasive voices from our past that run like tape recorders in our minds. Some hear the voice of a critical parent who frequently declared, "You'll never amount to anything!" Others benefit from the voice of a comforting parent who constantly reminded us of our worth and intelligence. Although we are often unaware of these voices, they have a powerful impact on our attitudes and actions.

Becoming aware of the numerous voices in our lives is the first step. The second is to figure out which ones emanate from God and which ones come from another source.

Is a particular incident in my life telling me something God wants me to know, or am I simply reading into it what I want to believe? Am I detecting God's urging through the advice of a friend, or am I simply hearing what I would like to hear and then claiming that it is divinely sanctioned? We yearn to detect God's guidance for our lives, yet we often find it difficult to distinguish between self-serving impulses and God's genuine nudges. How can we know? How can we become attuned to the whispers of God that seek to guide and transform us?

Think with me for a moment. When we hear a piece of music, whether it is a symphony or a song, we hear not only the individual notes but the overall pattern formed by the notes. If the music suddenly stops, a listener who is attuned to the pattern can anticipate how the music might continue. In a similar fashion, if we are attuned to God's pattern (God's nature and God's desires for our lives), we can better anticipate God's persuasive activity in our lives.

How do we become attuned to God's pattern? I believe we can begin to discern God's voice by spending time in silent reflection. Mahatma Gandhi, Martin Luther King Jr., and Mother Teresa have been widely recognized as being especially attuned to God. What enabled them to understand God's stirring in their lives? First, they expected to hear God's voice. Second, they became aware of the numerous influences in their lives. Third, by knowing God's pattern, they learned to distinguish between God's voice and contrary voices. Finally, and most important, each knew it was essential to spend time in solitude with God. On certain occasions they would consciously leave the busy world behind and spend time alone with God, seeking spiritual guidance.

Isn't this always true of those people who are most attuned to the persuasive activity of God? Moses ascended to the top of Mount Sinai for forty days to understand God's intentions for the Hebrew people. Jesus went into the wilderness for forty days before commencing his public ministry, and then at several significant junctures in his life he left his followers to be alone with God in prayer. Of course, forty days alone with God is well beyond our reach, but the tragedy is that forty minutes alone with God sounds like an eternity to most of us.

Although certain individuals have had unique and especially intense experiences of God, understanding God's pattern is not a great mystery reserved for a select few. God has no full-page ads, no prime-time commercials, no Web site, and no catchy jingles, but God does have the all-time best-seller. I believe the sacred writings of the Old and New Testaments reveal God's nature and desires for our lives. Over the centuries people have highlighted important scriptural themes. These help us determine those things that are in harmony with the desires of God and those things that are in opposition to God. *If we place these themes in the form of questions, we can test the influences in our lives to determine which are probably from God, and which have their origin in some other source.* Is the urging more likely to produce:

Acts of kindness and compassion	or	indifference
Harmony between people	or	dissension
Generosity toward others	or	selfishness
Justice	or	inequity
Truth	or	deception
Humility	or	arrogance
Respect for others and the natural world	or	contempt
Peace	or	strife?

God's persuasive power is like suggestive energy spoken to a place deep within us. Prayer, meditation, and silent reflection are the usual means by which we become aware of God's energetic touch. Thus, it is no great surprise that most of us are inept at recognizing God's stirring in our souls. The silent moments we spend reflecting on the people and events of our lives while listening for God's voice to emerge are practically nonexistent. We are constantly assaulted by outside stimuli, our calendars are crammed, and our pace of life is exhausting. We are experiencing information overload while simultaneously developing an insatiable appetite for being entertained. We have met the problem, and we are it. To be more precise, it is our lifestyle. Our way of living has driven moments of silence to the periphery of our lives. We have grown so used to the constant assault on our ears that many become restless and uncomfortable with silence. We think it is natural for something to be going on all the time—there has to be noise and there has to be motion. We are so used to racket and constant activity that most of us don't know much about being alone with God. In order to detect the whispers of God that offer us clarity and direction, it is essential for us to recapture quiet moments whose sole purpose is to focus our attention on what God is saying to us.

A passage in the Old Testament has always intrigued me. Generally in the Old Testament, when the writers tell us that God spoke to the people, they describe a very dramatic event—a burning bush, a pillar of smoke, thunder and lightning. But we cannot relate to such supernatural appearances of God because they are too foreign to the world in which we live. The story of the prophet Elijah however, reveals something akin to the way I believe we experience God.

Elijah has reached a desperate point in his life, and he has fled into the wilderness. He finds shelter in a cave, and while he is there, God speaks to him. We are told that there is a mighty wind, but God is not in the wind. Then comes an earthquake, but God is not in the earthquake. Next there is a fire, but God is not in the fire. Finally, we are told that there is "a sound of sheer silence." (The Hebrew actually says, "a sound of a gentle stillness.") And it is in the silence that Elijah discerns God's message to him.

The scene that I picture is Elijah being alone in the wilderness, reflecting on the people and events of his life and praying for some period of time to God for guidance. Then, in the awesome silence, he detects a stirring within himself that helps him to understand what God wants him to do.

And it works in the same fashion for us. When we experience difficult times and we are especially in need of God's guidance, we need to reflect on the people and events in our lives and to spend time in silence with God so that we can discern God's stirrings within our own souls.

One way to sharpen our awareness of the activity of God in our lives is to reflect in silence on the events of our day, identifying those moments we believe were in harmony with God's Spirit. We ask God to help us remember the satisfying moments when we felt that we were sharing something right and true and good with another person. These occasions are devoid of manipulation or insincerity and touch on the highest values in life—love, truth, peace, justice, and beauty. Often these episodes give us a feeling that this is the way life should be. These are moments when we are responding positively to the best possibility God is showing us. As we practice this technique, we find that it becomes easier to spot God's activity in our lives and, in turn, to become alert to other divine opportunities.

My friend Richard, the one who lost his leg in a dreadful accident, spent three months in the hospital and many more months at home healing. Throughout this period, he constantly exercised to strengthen his body. He also had a great deal of time alone with God. Time to think, time to pray, and time to listen.

Six years after his accident, Richard is back to living life to its fullest. He has traveled twice to Alaska to enjoy the rugged wilderness. On one of these adventures, he spent nine days on the Alaskan tundra camping in a tent, and on the first day of the trip he hiked ten miles. Later he said, "I got some blisters from my prosthesis. I guess I overdid it."

Some people never bounce back from such a tragedy. What made the difference with Richard? He credits two things with getting him through his ordeal and allowing him to return to a meaningful existence. He says the first was his belief that God was with him, helping him to heal. He kept experiencing a strong feeling that God would get him through his tragedy. He did not know how it would happen or what the outcome would be, but something deep inside made him believe that God would give him the strength, courage, and hope to face whatever would come. He asked me, "Do you remember that old commercial about the insurance company that said you would be in good hands with them? In my mind I kept seeing myself in the palms of God's hands."

The second thing that made the difference for Richard was that he had a goal. He was determined to enjoy once again the great outdoors, which had always given him a great deal of pleasure. Afraid that he would never be able to experience such pleasure again, he turned to God for strength and healing and determination so that he could again pursue his favorite pastime.

It's fair to ask what would have happened had Richard never been able to walk again. No one can know for certain. But Richard has a very strong faith, and I believe that if he had never been able to walk again, he would have prayed to God, "If I cannot do that again, then show me what I can do."

Richard returned to work and began to enjoy outdoor sports again. But it wasn't long before something unexpected bubbled up from within him. He began to have a growing desire to help others who were hurting. As a therapist, he had already been helping people for years, but this internal urge was prompting him to help others in a new and different way. For a while he was unsure what to do, but when his congregation announced that they wanted to train a few of their members to become "Stephen Ministers," Richard felt that this was what he was being persuaded to do. He then trained to become a caregiver, working with those who had lost a loved one, experienced a divorce, or had some other special need.

What was it that impelled Richard? He had been

through a difficult ordeal that had taken a heavy toll on him both physically and emotionally. Why would he choose to become involved in the emotionally taxing work of caring for people after office hours? Why not simply use any spare time in leisure activities?

After speaking with him, I had the strong feeling that he chose this path because God was encouraging him to help others in a specific way. I think God was urging him to use his personal experience with tragedy to touch the lives of others who faced difficult times.

God *desired* for Richard to do this, and God *urged* him to do this, but God did not *force* him to do this. The decision whether to embrace God's prompting or reject it was left up to Richard. And how does God work? In a variety of ways. It may be through the words of a friend—words that keep coming back to us when we spend time with God in silence. It may be an intuition that seems to move us in a particular direction. It may be through a passage of Scripture that continues to roll around in our minds and won't let go of us. Or it may be an event in our life that seems too pivotal to be a simple coincidence. If we believe one of these experiences to be the urging of God, we test it against what we know about the pattern of God.

It is important to point out that God did not suddenly present Richard with the possibility of becoming a Stephen Minister in a way that was striking and clearly apparent to him. In the days immediately following the accident, God was not urging him to become involved in a ministry to others. This option evolved from a lengthy process of small, subtle urgings. As in Richard's life, it is easier to form conclusions about God's activity in our own lives after some time has passed and we can look back on a situation. Once things have worked to a particular outcome, it is easier to reflect on the steps that helped us reach it and to identify ways in which God was involved. If the situation has reached a positive conclusion, we may assume that we were receptive—at least for the most part—to God's urgings. If the situation did not reach a favorable result, we may detect key places where we ignored God's persuasive activity. Each time we reflect on the various steps of an important situation in our lives—with an eye toward detecting God's activity—we improve our awareness of those moments when God is seeking to persuade us.

It seems apparent that from the moment Richard was struck by the car, God was actively involved in his life, presenting possibilities for healing. Some of these involved the many people who played a part in helping him recover, and some involved Richard himself. Each possibility took into account the current situation and built on it.

Initially the possibilities were simply for survival. For two weeks following the accident, Richard lay in the intensive care unit drifting in and out of consciousness. During this time in ICU, his wife and children, as well as several doctors and nurses, were attending to his needs, but he has no conscious memory of any of them. He remembers only three people who touched his life— two ministers and one nurse.

His very first memory following the accident is of seeing one of his ministers (an older man with white hair) standing over him and smiling. Richard thought he was in heaven and said to himself, "If this is what heaven is like, it's going to be good!"

Today Richard is embarrassed that he cannot remember seeing his wife and children during the days he was in ICU. After all, these are the people he loves best and cares about most. But I think he remembers the ministers and the nurse because they were symbols of God. I believe they represented God's presence and hope. These were critical for Richard's recovery while his body was still in trauma.

Once the danger of death had passed, God touched Richard's life by presenting possibilities that were aimed at the quality of life he could expect. Three things were especially difficult for Richard. First, he wrestled with what he could no longer do physically. Even though Richard knew in his head that he could not do certain things, a part of him intensely resisted the thought that he had a permanent disability. Second, he had to face the fact that his body was irrevocably altered. One of his legs was gone forever. Third, he had to become dependent on others. Richard had always been an independent person who was comfortable giving aid to others. For weeks following the accident, he found himself entirely dependent on others for the most basic functions of life.

While Richard grieved what he had lost, I presume God was encouraging him to embrace a new existence—the best that was possible given the situation. Richard did not latch on to it immediately, but over time he gradually reformed his image of himself and his possible future. The physical therapists helped him confront his altered body, and the love and encouragement of his family played a key role in helping him grasp the possibilities before him.

I assume God presented possibilities for developing in Richard an ever-stronger spirit of determination to withstand the discomfort and to undertake the rigorous exercises. His physical therapists challenged him, and something inside of him (I'd call it God's urging) deepened his resolve to keep trying and hoping rather than giving up in despair.

Along the way, Richard recognized other signs that gave him reason to be hopeful about the future. Two young children—unknown to Richard—played prominent roles in helping him achieve the full life he now lives. The first was a nine-year-old girl whom he saw several times during the months he lived in a rehabilitation clinic. The little girl would be in the clinic lobby, and Richard would notice her eyeing him whenever he came by. The first two months he was wheeled through the lobby in a wheelchair. Then he progressed to using a walker on one leg. Finally, he was using a walker with a prosthesis. Shortly after that, the little girl knocked on the door of his room. She came in and said, "Mister, this was a miracle. I didn't know God made legs grow back."

Of course, adults know that God does not make legs regenerate. Richard could have been bitter and responded to God with anger for not making his leg grow back or for not preventing the accident in the first place. Instead, this proved to be a watershed experience for him. He decided that the girl was communicating a vital message to him. Her words kept ringing in his ears until he decided that she was right. "It was a miracle," Richard says to this day, "I'm alive and I'm walking."

The second child who played a pivotal role was a boy he never met. Not far from the site of Richard's accident is an elementary school, and one of the fourth-grade teachers asked her students to write letters "to the man who was hurt in the accident." The letters arrived while he was in the rehabilitation clinic, and one of the letters touched him deeply. A little boy wrote simply, "My dog got hit by a car and he's doing fine so I'm sure you will be fine." Richard chuckles about the naive notion of the child but says that the letter resonated with something deep within him that was saying, "This is true. You will be fine." I believe this strong internal feeling of which Richard became aware was the voice of God.

As Richard's health improved and he returned to work, he began to feel a sense of gratitude like he had never known before. Rather than feeling sorry for himself because of his new limitations, he felt incredibly thankful for having survived his ordeal and being able to rebuild a fulfilling life. Coupled with the feelings of thankfulness was an urge that Richard felt was coming from God to become involved in a special ministry to others. He considered this possibility for some time, pondering the details of what such a commitment would entail and weighing it against other options. Eventually he decided to undergo the training and become a Stephen Minister. I believe he responded to the best possibility God presented to him, and that is why he is so enthusiastic about his life today.

When we look at what has happened to Richard from the time of his accident to the present, I believe we can see examples of how God was active in his life. At times Richard detected God's voice through certain people he encountered, and at times God's voice was an internal feeling or intuition. I believe God acts in a similar fashion in everyone's life. God seeks to persuade us to the best possibility for our lives given the situation, speaking to us through people, events, and internal feelings.

In *Traveling Mercies* Anne Lamott explains a very dark period in her life that lasted several years, and the steps that led her out of it. As with Richard, there were key people who helped her find a new existence. In addition, she describes a critical juncture: "But in my dark bedroom at Pat's that afternoon, out of nowhere it crossed my mind to call the new guy at St. Stephen's."[14] The "new guy" was an Episcopal minister who became a very important counselor for her. What caught my attention was how she decided to go to him for help. She said, ". . . out of nowhere it crossed my mind." I have heard many people use that phrase to describe an impulse they had to do something that turned out to be a critical event for them. As you might guess, I don't think the idea came from "out of nowhere." I think it was most likely a "whisper" from God. I believe all of us experience these urgings. It is up to us to discern what God is communicating to us and then to respond positively. How do we do this?

Again, to summarize: First, we must expect to hear God's voice. Reflecting on the people and the events of our lives, we must be alert to the possibilities that are constantly before us. Second, we must be aware of the numerous influences in our lives. Some are internal and some are external; some are from God and some are not. Third, we must become familiar with God's pattern in order to distinguish between God's voice and contrary voices. And finally, we must leave our noisy and busy lives behind to spend time in solitude with God. In silence, we reflect on the people and events of our lives and ask God for guidance. As we do, we begin to detect stirrings within our soul. We can test these various influences to determine which ones are in harmony with God, keeping in mind that God never stops presenting us with possibilities that will transform our lives. God does not create situations by controlling people. Rather, God envisions the best possibilities and then urges us to embrace them.

CHAPTER NINE

Life After Death?

If we have experienced deep pain and suffering through a devastating loss, we may firmly believe that the future holds little more than painful memories and dreams cut short. However, it is essential for us to realize that our lives are not destined to end in despair. The future is open, and God seeks to guide us to the best life possible given our circumstances.

Knowing that God is working for our best possible future gives us hope that our pain will subside even though our loss will always be with us, as well as hope that we will have new opportunities to experience joy and fulfillment. However, what makes this life worth living and the future truly bright is the hope that we will one day be reunited with our loved ones who have perished.

The transforming power of God makes new life possible. I believe God's power makes new life possible not only during our earthly existence but also *beyond this life*.

Some say that belief in life after death is a quaint idea tantamount to wishful thinking. Or they say that such a belief is maintained by only biblical literalists. However, I believe that the end of our earthly lives is not the end of our existence, and I believe there are solid reasons for maintaining hope in life after death.

In one of his letters to the church in Corinth, the Apostle Paul wrote these eloquent words:

For if the dead are not raised, then Christ has not been raised. If Christ has not been raised, your faith is futile and you are still in your sins. Then those also who have died in Christ have perished. If for this life only we have hoped in Christ, we are of all people most to be pitied. But in fact Christ has been raised from the dead, the firstfruits of those who have died. For since death came through a human being, the resurrection of the dead has also come through a human being; for as all die in Adam, so all will be made alive in Christ. (I Corinthians 15:16–22)

If we can honestly believe in life after death, we will discover a hope and peace of mind that makes life worth living. I believe this life is only the beginning of a much wider experience that continues to unfold.

One day our physical bodies will die, and if we are not cremated, our flesh and bones will eventually break down into basic elements. I often recite, while conducting a committal service at the gravesite, "earth to earth, ashes to ashes, dust to dust." However, as the Apostle Paul explains in the fifteenth chapter of the First Letter to the Corinthians, "this perishable body must put on imperishability, and this mortal body must put on immortality." That is, our physical nature may be no more, but our new transformed spiritual nature will live eternally with God. Sounds wonderful, but in our age of hard facts, is it plausible for us to maintain such a belief?

The modern world, with its emphasis on the objective observation of physical data, has cast such doubt on the idea of life after death that a great number of people have become highly skeptical of the belief that life continues beyond the grave. After all, it is a basic fact that you can dig up the grave of someone who has been buried and the remains of the person will still be inside the casket. You can cast your eyes on them. Museums display exhibits in which it is possible to observe the remains of persons who died thousands of years ago. Many believe that if this is not absolute proof, it may be at least an arrow pointing in the direction of skepticism. Although many would not be too uncomfortable discussing life after death in a church school class on a Sunday morning, they would hesitate to bring up this subject in a social gathering with people who have no religious affiliation. We might be concerned that people would raise their eyebrows and think to themselves, "How naive!"

This pervading climate of skepticism concerning life after death has been with us for much of the twentieth century. The exciting news is that over the last few years the climate has begun to change. Now we are beginning to hear talk of life after death from people who strongly embrace the basic premises of modern science. Although the voices beginning to speak out are still in the minority, their number is increasing, and what they have to say can be understood in terms that make sense to rational, thinking people.

Dr. Bernie Siegel is one of those voices. He is a surgeon in New Haven, Connecticut, and teaches at Yale University. In his best-selling book *Love, Medicine, and Miracles*, Dr. Siegel shares how his work with cancer patients has made him aware of the great difference between those cancer patients who have a spiritual life and those who do not. He discovered what recent independent studies have confirmed: Patients who possess an active religious faith *are more likely to get well* than those who do not. In addition, these patients are more likely to be at peace if their death becomes imminent.

Dr. Siegel forms support groups with cancer patients in which the group members share openly and honestly with one another. He creates an atmosphere in which "you can talk about anything you desire, and it doesn't matter how crazy it might sound."[15] One of the things he discovered is that once people feel free to share *anything*, many say that they have experienced communication from people who have already died.

On numerous occasions, he has heard stories about persons who knew of a close relative's death *before* actually receiving news of it. Dr. Siegel's father told of the time when he was a young man and his mother visited him in spirit one day at work. She said good-bye to him. He knew at that moment that his mother had died, and he grew terribly sad. His coworkers noticed, but he could not tell them what had happened because it sounded too bizarre. However, as soon as he reached home the telephone rang, and his sister informed him that their mother had died.[16]

Dr. Siegel has heard many similar stories from his patients. Once they discovered that Dr. Siegel's father had experienced communication from someone who had died, they felt free to share their own stories.

I have never personally experienced communication from someone who died, but a few church members have shared such stories with me. I confess that when I heard their stories I was quite skeptical. Having received a fair amount of training in the field of counseling, I automatically processed the stories in psychological terms: "There is probably some wish fulfillment going on. There might be some delusion as this person struggles to find a way to cope with her loved one's death." I thought only in psychological terms when I should have also been thinking in theological terms.

Related to after-death communication is the experience of people who have died and then been revived. I have known two individuals who were clinically dead and then resuscitated; both told me the details of their experiences. Although these two people never knew each other, I was struck by the similarities of what they experienced. Both were undergoing medical procedures when their hearts stopped, and both described being outside their physical bodies and hovering above the table where doctors and nurses were working on their bodies. Both said that they experienced an incredible sense of peace such as they had never experienced before or since. Both clearly heard every word spoken by the physicians, who were working frantically on their bodies trying to "bring them back," and both even told the doctors about it later, quoting them word for word. Neither individual had been the least bit anxious to return to their physical body, and in fact, both said they felt somewhat hesitant to return. Each made reference to a bright light, and both proclaim very calmly and confidently that they now have absolutely no fear of death because they are keenly aware as never before that something very peaceful and satisfying awaits them.

At one time in my life, I based my belief in life after death on the assertion that there are some things you simply have to take on faith. But as my faith has evolved over the years, I no longer rely on that response. Too many times in the past I used it as a cop-out. I'm not comfortable with that response because it implies that faith is opposed to reason. But faith and reason do not need to be mutually exclusive. Because I believe that God is the Creator of all that exists, my religious faith should be in harmony with what the scientific community discovers about the world. Thus, my belief in life after death is now based primarily on my religious faith, but my belief also squares with what I know about human existence.

Think with me for a moment. In one sense, we are physical beings. We are made of flesh and bones and muscle and blood and organs, but that is not all we are. To think of ourselves only as *physical* creatures is limiting. We are also something else.

In our home we enjoy taking photographs of special occasions, and we define "special occasions" very loosely. Almost any occasion can merit a few photographs, and as a result we have a large number of photo albums swollen with pictures. I pull out four photographs of myself and set them on the table before me. The first one is a picture my parents snapped shortly after bringing me home for the first time from the hospital. In my youth I found this to be a humiliating photograph, and I would have died had any of my peers seen it. I am stark naked and lying in the middle of the dining room table. You may wonder why my parents took such a picture—I wonder the same thing—but that is not the point. The point is that I was tiny. Very tiny. I weighed slightly over six pounds, and I was about twenty inches long. At this stage I was totally dependent on others. In time I learned to crawl, then walk. I learned that words represent things. But lying there on that dining room table, I was basically helpless.

Next to my baby picture I place a photograph of myself at age ten in my Cub Scout uniform with a big grin and a face full of freckles. I was much larger than in the nude baby shot, but I was still an average young boy. The third photograph on the table before me is from my football-playing days at Kansas State University. I was twenty years old and over six feet tall, had a seventeen-inch neck, and weighed 220 pounds. The difference between the first and third photographs is astounding. In the first one, I am a mere centerpiece on the table, and in the third one, I am about the size of the table. It is hard to believe that each photograph was taken of the same person.

Finally, I have a fourth photograph before me: a recent picture taken last Christmas. The most noticeable difference is that I have a great deal less hair than in my earlier days! Also, in spite of the fact that I weigh less than in college, I'm not nearly as well conditioned.

Gazing at these four photographs reveals radical differences in my size and shape and age. I appear very different in each one, yet I know that each of them is me. In addition to the changes I can plainly see, I am aware that scientists have discovered that all of the cells in our bodies replace themselves every seven years, so literally I am a different physical being in each of the photos. Yet despite being a completely different physical entity in each of these stages of my life, there is a link that connects them all. There is something about me that transcends the physical differences, enabling my parents to say of each photograph, "That's Greg!"

I can remember things I did ten years ago, twenty years ago, thirty years ago, even forty years ago. There is something about me that is not physical, and has endured from the time I entered this world. I'm not sure what the best term is for this thing that is me but not physically me. We might refer to it as *spirit* or *essence* or *soul*. The point is, there is something about each of us that is not physical and that endures throughout our lifetime. And if it is not physical, then why couldn't it continue on even *after* the physical part of us dies?

Certainly it could. In fact, once it is released from the body, with its aches and pains and physical limitations, why couldn't the spirit become greater than it ever was within material restraints? In fact, once we are freed from the constant stimulation of our physical body—through sight, sound, smell, and so on—why couldn't our perception of both our past experiences and our new experiences be more intense than ever before? It very well could. And doesn't this square with reports we have heard from people who have died and been resuscitated? Often they speak of a dramatic review of their life ("I saw my whole life flash in front of me") and an experience of a bright light (or something they perceived to be God).

If we believe that nothing exists apart from that which is physical, then belief in life after death is problematic. But if we acknowledge that there is also reality that is not limited to what the five senses can perceive, then life after death becomes a viable possibility.

A few years ago my wife's mother died, and my wife and I had the privilege of spending her final days with her. When the end finally came, she was ready to go, and we had the opportunity to say all of our good-byes more than once. Her mother was tired of being in bed, in pain, and constantly short of breath, and she was looking forward to joining her husband, who had died seven years earlier. But a few days before she died, something very unusual occurred. My wife and I received a phone call in the middle of the night from a nurse who said that we had better come quickly to her bedside because the nurse believed she was about to die. We were only four miles from her and knew we could be there in a short time. My wife and I dressed very quickly, I put in my contact lenses and grabbed a glass of milk, and we headed for the door. However, as we were walking out the door the telephone rang again. It had been only five minutes since the first call, but the nurse was much more frantic this time. "You'd better get here as fast as you can! I don't know how much longer she can last."

We arrived in a matter of minutes to find my mother-in-law surrounded by a nurse and two aides who were frantically monitoring her vital signs. We're not exactly sure what happened over the next twenty minutes or so, but we believe my mother-in-law went to the brink of death, peered through to the other side of existence, and then returned. Her face was unlike anything we have ever seen before. My wife and I have fumbled for words to describe it, but nothing seems to adequately portray what we witnessed. The words *glowing* and *radiant* come close but are still lacking. Her mother's face was actually a different color. It wasn't ghostly or pale, but rather bright and beaming. It wasn't yellow, but sort of white-gold.

Not only did her countenance take on an extraordinary appearance, but a shiny film covered her teeth and her eyes sparkled with intensity. She was looking up and away from us and appeared to be focused not on the ceiling but beyond it. She began calling out names of numerous family members and friends, all of whom are deceased. At first we thought she was trying to tell us whom she was looking forward to seeing once she died, which appeared to be about to happen any moment. But in a short while, both of us had the distinct feeling that she was not thinking about whom she hoped to see, but about the people *she was actually seeing at that moment*. As she called out each name, her smile grew and she became more and more excited, at times almost laughing. I lost all sense of time, but I would guess this episode lasted twenty or thirty minutes. Throughout this time, my wife kept telling her mother how much she loved her and what a wonderful mother she had been. I read passages of Scripture to her that I knew she would find comforting. Throughout this intense experience, we were anticipating that at any moment she would breathe her last breath. However, that moment did not come, and after a while her appearance gradually returned to normal.

The nurse and aides had no idea what was going on! Later, in the hallway, one of the aides who had been next to the bed during the episode said in a very soft voice to me, "I've never seen anything like that before."

The nurse who had been monitoring her throughout the ordeal was visibly shaken. I found her seated at a table outside the nurses' station shaking her head and staring at my mother-in-law's chart. She kept saying over and over that she had never seen anyone whose vital signs had dropped so low and not died.

I cannot say with certainty what actually occurred that night. Nobody who was in that room can. But all of us who were present know that something exceptional took place. Was my wife's mother having delusions, or did she really see her loved ones? No one can give a conclusive answer. She lived only three more days after the extraordinary event, but in those final days not only did she exhibit no signs of fear or apprehension about death, but she was eagerly anticipating what seemed to be about to happen to her. I believe she knew that she was about to be liberated from her wornout physical body, and that something splendid awaited her.

Very few people have the opportunity to experience what we believe my wife's mother experienced—to see through to the other side and receive the assurance that something joyous awaits us and we need not fear the end of our earthly physical existence. However, the numbers are increasing. With the continuing advances of medical technology, more and more people have been brought back to life after dying. They share very powerful stories of something extraordinary occurring to them that convinces them that the end of their *physical* existence is not the end of their total existence. Many of these people live the remainder of their lives with a firm conviction that another realm—the spiritual—awaits them.

Although our bodies eventually give out, marking the end of our earthly, physical existence, it is not the end for us. We are more than physical beings. We have a spiritual nature that exists beyond this earthly existence. After we die, God resurrects or transforms or recreates our spiritual nature in a form that in some ways resembles our physical appearance yet in some ways differs from it. I believe that those we have known during our time on earth will be able to recognize us in the next life —whether they knew us as a child, teenager, middle-aged person, or old person.

Dr. John Vanarsdall once related the following story. Around 1800 a child named John Todd was born in Vermont, and when he was six years old, both of his parents died and all the children had to be divided up among various relatives. Little John was sent to live with an aunt whom he had never seen, but she ended up taking exceptional care of him. She put him through college and saw him into his chosen profession. After he had become a grown man, word came to John that this dear aunt was seriously ill and on the verge of death. She was in mortal terror of the prospect. Since he could not go to her bedside personally, he wrote these words to her in a letter:

It is now thirty-five years since I, a little boy of six, was left quite alone in the world. I have never forgotten that day when I made the long journey to your house in North Killingsworth. I still recall how you sent your hired man, Caesar, to fetch me. And I can still remember my tears and anxiety as, perched on your horse and clinging tightly to Caesar's back, I started out for my new home. As we rode along, I became more and more afraid, and finally said to Caesar, "Do you think she will go to bed before we get there?" "Oh, no," he said reassuringly. "When we get out of these here woods, you will see her candle shining in the window." In a short time, we did ride out into a clearing, and there, sure enough, was your candle. I still remember the sight of you waiting at the door, how you put out your arms to me and lifted me down from the horse. I remember there was a fire on your hearth, a warm supper on your stove, and after supper, you took me up to bed, heard my prayers and then sat beside me until I dropped off to sleep. You undoubtedly realize why I am recalling all these things just now. Some day soon, God may send for you to take you to a new home. Do not fear that summons, and do not fear the strange journey or the messenger of death. At the end of that road you will find love and welcome. You will be safe in God's love and care. Surely God can be trusted to be as kind to you there as you were to me years ago.[17]

Written over a century ago, this letter captures the belief that something wonderful awaits us after our physical existence on earth comes to an end.

Belief in life after death enables us to live our lives with genuine hope following the loss of a loved one. And authentic hope produces in us an optimistic attitude that enhances the quality of our present existence. Joy and meaning can return to our lives today. We can continue to grow and be enriched, and life can once again become fulfilling and worthwhile.

A colleague shared a story he had read about John Quincy Adams. One day shortly before his eightieth birthday, Adams was hobbling down the street in Boston, leaning rather heavily on his cane. A friend tapped the elderly gentleman on the shoulder and asked, "Well, how is John Quincy Adams this morning?" The old man turned toward his friend very slowly, a smile broke across his face, and he replied, "Fine, sir, fine! But this old tenement that John Quincy lives in is not doing so well. The underpinning is about to fall away. The thatch is all gone off the roof, and the windows are so dim John Quincy can hardly see out anymore. As a matter of fact, it wouldn't surprise me if before the winter's over he had to move out. But as for John Quincy Adams, he never was better . . . never was better!"[18]

This life is not all there is. There is something more, something beyond the grave.

❖

Moving from Grief
to Cherished Memories

Our hope in eternal life can be the key to healing the pain, the sadness, and the despair of grief. The belief that our loved ones no longer suffer and the expectation that we will one day be reunited with them can bring joy back into our lives. However, we would be mistaken to expect this to occur quickly. Before we are able fully to embrace the hope of a future reunion with those who have died, we must first grieve their current absence from our lives. Although we have hope for the future, we experience pain in the present. How do we make it through such difficult times? In addition to our belief in eternal life, what else is there to help us successfully navigate our course through the deep waters of grief?

If you fracture your leg, the doctor can tell you that you will be in a cast for six weeks; once the cast is removed, you will go through a set period of physical therapy, and then the doctor will pronounce your leg fully healed. For a given period of time your leg is injured, and then at some point it is healed. Grief is not as tidy, nor is the length of time as predictable. When we experience a serious loss, the pain and sadness come and go. There is no set duration. We may begin to feel better and think that our time of grieving is complete; then the sadness comes back, and we realize that we are not finished. Someone once told me that her grief was like the tide of the ocean. It comes in and goes out, over and over again. That's a pretty good analogy, except for one difference—you can accurately predict the tides. Not so with grief. You might be feeling fine for days, then you stop by the grocery store to pick up a few items and see something that triggers emotions within you. Perhaps it's nothing more than a box of cereal that was your loved one's favorite, but suddenly something comes over you and tears begin to flow. You think you will totally fall apart if you don't rush out of the store immediately. Grief is like that—it's unpredictable, and you never know what might set it off.

If you experience a loss, it is important for you to know the stages of grief through which people pass. This provides you with a gauge against which you can check yourself. You may be experiencing thoughts and feelings you have never had before, yet if you are familiar with the commonly delineated stages of grief, you may find that your experience is similar to that of others who have grieved a serious loss. Despite how peculiar you may feel, what is going on inside you is normal.

A number of years ago, Elisabeth Kübler-Ross did pioneering work in the field of grief, and she helped us to understand better what we might expect when we grieve a serious loss. For instance, when we first receive terrible news—such as the sudden death of a loved one—our initial response is often denial. We cannot believe what we are hearing. We say things such as, "Surely there has been a mistake," or, "I just can't believe it." The pain is so severe that we cannot fully absorb the harsh news. I have known several people who experienced the death of a loved one, went through the motions of a visitation, funeral, and graveside service, and then later remarked that it did not seem real to them. It is not uncommon to hear people say that the first few days following a tragedy seemed like a bad dream.

It is essential for you to know that your goal is not to attempt to put your loss out of your mind—that is a form of denial. Rather, your goal is to be able eventually to accept what has happened and to learn how to live with your loss. You cannot achieve this goal immediately because it is too painful. You must work your way through the various stages of grief, moving forward, falling back, moving forward again, until you discover how to live with your loss.

Glenn dropped by his church to speak with the minister. A few weeks earlier Glenn's teenage son had died in a terrible automobile accident that had left others injured, and he was struggling to handle the trauma. He said to his pastor, "I'm having difficulty concentrating at work. I'll be involved in a project, and the next thing I know I'm staring into space, thinking about my son. I keep trying to put the painful memories out of my mind, but they keep reappearing. I'll never be able to forget what happened."

This is exactly as it should be. When suffering the loss of a loved one, the goal is not to forget—that is a form of denial. The goal is to accept what has happened and the pain of the loss, because once we accept what has occurred, we can ponder it without *dwelling* on it. However, it is essential to keep in mind that acceptance does not come quickly or easily.

Depending on the circumstances surrounding the death of your loved one, the period of grief can be somewhat mild and brief or extremely intense and prolonged. After conducting the funeral for someone who has lived a long, full life, I find that the length of time for loved ones to grieve deeply is generally a year or so. However, following a funeral for someone who has died before she has grown old, the heartache is much more pronounced and can last for years.

When a tragedy first strikes, you may find yourself in a state of shock and denial. Eventually the shock begins to wear off, the reality of the tragedy begins to sink in, and the intensity of the pain increases. Along with the pain often comes anger.

A colleague told me about Miriam, who had come to him for counseling. Her eighteen-year-old son had been killed by a drunk driver, and as expected, Miriam was having a very difficult time handling the tragedy. Well-meaning friends at work had cautioned her not to talk about it because that would be too upsetting for her. (Actually it was too upsetting for *them*.) A couple of her friends from church told her she was obligated "to forgive the driver." (Apparently it did not dawn on them that forgiveness would take more time—if it ever came.) Miriam needed to talk, and she was nowhere near the point of forgiving the drunk driver. She was filled with rage. But rather than finding constructive ways to release it, she felt guilty for feeling angry. She could not bring herself to admit it, but she was furious with her friends at work, with her church friends, and especially with God. Miriam wanted to know why God would allow such a terrible tragedy. Her son had perished, the drunk driver had survived. Why not the other way around? But, she told my colleague over and over, she could not give voice to these feelings because she was afraid God would inflict more pain on her.

Since God loves us and accepts us for who we are, it's all right to be angry with God. We can have a totally open and honest relationship with God that might include venting our fury. God will not reject us because we get mad and rage on, and God does not "teach us lessons" by taking the lives of those we love. Listen to these words from Psalm 13: "How long, O Lord? Will you forget me forever? How long will you hide your face from me? How long must I bear pain in my soul, and have sorrow in my heart all day long? How long shall my enemy be exalted over me?" Or these words from the prophet Jeremiah: "Why does the way of the guilty prosper? Why do all who are treacherous thrive?" (12:1). That is essentially the same question the woman was asking. Why does a drunk driver get away with it? Neither the psalmist nor Jeremiah is pleased with the way things are going, and they do not hesitate to take their complaint to God. They know they can bare their soul honestly and straightforwardly. Their terse language does not damage their ties with God.

Do you ever get angry with your children? I do occasionally, but there is never a doubt that I love my children dearly. In fact, if I never became angry with them, it would not be a sign of deeper love but rather of apathy. I believe God would prefer us to be angry with him than to be totally indifferent.

When we are in the midst of grief, it is important for us to face squarely the fury that rages deep within us, and we need to take that strong emotion to God. If we ignore the fury, it is likely to seep out in cruel or destructive ways. It may take the form of sharp words toward our family and friends; it may take the shape of excessive drinking or compulsive eating. If you are married, it will probably create the most intense strain ever placed on your bond of love.

In the Old Testament story of Job, after he had been devastated by continual tragedy and argued with his friends, telling them that he did not deserve what had happened to him, Job took his complaint to God. Listen to what he said: "And now my soul is poured out within me; days of affliction have taken hold of me. The night racks my bones, and the pain that gnaws me takes no rest. . . . I cry to you and you do not answer me; I stand, and you merely look at me. You have turned cruel to me; with the might of your hand you persecute me. You lift me up on the wind, you make me ride on it, and you toss me about in the roar of the storm. I know that you will bring me to death, and to the house appointed for all living" (30:16, 17, 20–23).

The blunt language we find in Scripture leads me to believe that there is no need for us to tiptoe around God. It is not necessary for us to limit our prayers to pleasant words and pious phrases. God already knows the feelings we have within us; we might as well admit them to ourselves. Once we have done this, we can trust God to help us plow through our anger and to help us find healing from our pain. Nearly everyone I know who has suffered the loss of a child has told me that sometimes when they are alone, they yell and scream with all their might. At times their screaming is directed at God. They say that their screaming helps; they don't know why, but it does.

In addition to facing our anger and finding constructive ways to handle it, we may also need to deal with feelings of guilt. Some people compound their grief by also carrying a burden of guilt. Keep in mind that guilt comes in different shapes. There is constructive guilt, and there is destructive guilt. Constructive guilt prods us to act in ways that respect ourselves and others. We *should* feel guilty if we take something that does not belong to us, or if we do something to violate the trust of another, or if we do something that harms another physically or emotionally. Constructive guilt helps us to distinguish between right and wrong behavior. Destructive guilt is something else. It has a negative outcome. It tears down rather than builds up. People who grieve the loss of a loved one commonly berate themselves for not having done something to prevent the death. They provoke feelings of guilt by blaming themselves for what has occurred.

For months a mother suffered tremendous guilt after the death of her child. She had not checked the back-door of her car to ensure that it was locked. Her older children told her it was locked, but apparently it was not. Her toddler fell out of the car and was killed. She tormented herself for a long period of time, but eventually she developed an outlook that would be good for anyone to have. She said, "I asked myself, if I had my child back, could I promise that I would never make another mistake? I knew I could not make that promise."[19] None of us can make that promise. If the day you would like to change could be undone, what about the next day and the next? We cannot berate ourselves continuously saying, "If only I had done this." That sort of guilt gets us nowhere and eats away at our soul until we destroy ourselves.

Some people experience guilt when their prayers are not answered. Stephen confided, "What's wrong with me? I must be doing something wrong. My mother is unconscious, with no hope of recovery, and yet she continues to suffer. Each day I pray over and over for God to take her, to alleviate her suffering, but she continues to linger. What am I doing wrong? Sometimes I feel like God is punishing me for something I've done."

I know a woman, Abigail, who gave birth to a daughter with severe retardation. As if the trials of raising her child were not enough, the mother tormented herself with the notion that this was God's way of punishing her. Abigail believed God was punishing her for an abortion she had undergone two years prior to the birth

of this child (even though her doctor had strongly rec-
ommended the abortion).

Both of these people were destroying themselves with
guilt for no good reason. The problem was that both of
them were blaming themselves for things beyond their
control. The issue was not *them*. The issue was God's
power. More specifically, the issue was the kind of power
God possesses. I have to believe that if God could have
ended the elderly woman's suffering sooner, God would
have done that. Also, I simply cannot fathom God punishing parents by seeing to it that their child is born with
mental retardation. God is loving and merciful and wants
the best for us, but there are some things that God cannot
do because God's power is persuasive, not controlling.

Some people do not feel guilty for a tragedy, but then
are invaded by a feeling of guilt as the darkness begins to
lift and they begin to feel better. They feel guilty for
feeling *good*. They imagine that they are supposed to
continue feeling terrible. C. S. Lewis, working through
his grief following the death of his wife, spoke of the
time when his darkness began to lift. He said that when
he began to feel better, he immediately felt ashamed. He
felt as if he were somehow obligated to cherish and to
foster and to prolong his sadness.[20] Guilt can slowly
destroy us.

It should become evident to us how much we need
other people. We need individuals who can genuinely

listen to us without being judgmental and without letting their own agenda get in the way. We need at least one person with whom we can be totally honest and share our thoughts regardless of how bizarre they may sound. Also, we must allow other people to do nice things for us. We need to let people bring us a meal, write us a note, run an errand for us. We need someone to help us vent our anger, and we need someone to help us work through our feelings of guilt. Their kindness shows us that we are valued and worth caring for. In addition, we need someone to remind us that God forgives us, and therefore we must be able to forgive ourselves. Those who are active members of a religious community often discover the critical support they need to move forward with their lives. If the members of our community of faith are loving and sensitive to our pain, they can support us as we move through our grief.

However, it is unrealistic to expect our friends to know automatically what we need. Most people have no idea what to do with someone who has lost a loved one. As uncomfortable as this may sound, you may have to tell people what you need and what you don't need. Tell people that you would like for them simply to spend time with you without feeling compelled to say only the right things to make you feel better. Sometimes we need a person's presence but not her advice or explanations. Rabbi Harold Kushner tells the story of a little boy who was sent on an errand by his mother. The little boy was gone much longer than expected, and the mother began to worry. Finally he came back home, and the mother asked him, "Where were you? I was very worried about you!" And the little boy replied, "There was this boy down the street who was crying because his bicycle was broken. I felt bad for him, so I stopped to help him." The mother said, "But you don't know anything about fixing a bicycle." And the little boy answered, "I know that. I didn't fix his bike. I sat down with him, and I helped him cry."[21]

When we have experienced a tragedy, words of explanation rarely comfort us. In moments like these, there are no gems of wisdom that can be shared with us to make us feel better. We certainly do not need to hear the trite phrase "It must be God's will." But there is something people can do to help. They can be physically present with us. They can sit down with us and help us cry.

In addition, they can listen to us. Perhaps the most valuable gift a friend can give us when we have suffered a painful loss is to be an attentive listener. It is essential for us to put into words what has happened to us and how we're feeling about it. In the initial stages of our loss, articulating what has occurred enables us to work through our denial and to realize it's not simply a bad dream, it is real. Once we have worked through our denial, it is necessary for us to talk about what has happened because as we converse about our loss we come to a better understanding of what it actually means for our lives. This does not come into focus quickly or easily. There is something about grief that produces a strong desire within us to talk about our loss many times. It would be ideal if we could talk about our feelings and share our story once or twice with a sympathetic listener and then move on, but it doesn't work that way. In fact, we are likely to discover that we experience a compelling need to recite our story over and over.

A woman in my congregation whose husband had died came to me for counseling for several months. During each session she told me what had happened and its impact on her life. On each occasion she narrated the story as if she hadn't already told me. The truth is, she had related her story to me so many times that I could remind her if she failed to mention certain details. It even reached the point where she would pause in the midst of her story and say, "I know I've told you this before, but . . ." and then she would launch back into her story without missing a beat. It finally reached the point that I began thinking to myself, "I don't know if I can stand to hear the same thing one more time! She must move beyond this." Fortunately, the next time she came to talk, she said, "You know, I'm tired of repeating the same thing time after time. For some reason I just had to keep telling the story. Now I'm tired of telling it. Maybe that means I've finally accepted it deep down inside of me." She taught me a tremendous lesson. After the death of a loved one, we need patient listeners who can hear our story over and over until we grow weary of telling it.

In the early stages of our grief, it is important to have people who genuinely listen to us and share the burden of our pain. We do not need to hear explanations that attempt to explain why our tragedy occurred. In addition, it is very helpful when people mention our loved one who has died. It is especially comforting to hear about the ways in which our loved one made a positive impact on the life of another. Unfortunately, people unknowingly compound our pain by failing to speak of our loved one. Most people are timid about mentioning our dear departed for fear of deepening or prolonging our sadness. We may need to inform them that their silence is even more painful.

I knew a woman whose son had died in his twenties. She told me that one of the things that bothered her most was that her friends would never talk about him or mention his name. She was deeply hurt, because "they acted as if he never existed."

Michael Lindvall, a Presbyterian minister, recalls a crazy childhood memory that dropped into his head one day when he was questioning the significance of his life.

He said it seemed like "a dark parable for life itself." When he was six or seven years old, he watched a children's television program called *Axel's Tree House*. This was live, local programming in the early fifties. The show was quite unpredictable, unrehearsed, and unprofessional. Axel was an old man, or at least that's how Lindvall remembers him. (He was probably all of forty.) He lived in a tree house and spoke, for some inexplicable reason, with a fake Swedish accent. Several times during the show, Axel would peer through a telescope and say, "I tink I see dem Little Rascals out dere." And with that, a Little Rascals adventure would appear on the screen.

At both the beginning and the end of each show, the camera would pan to a small set of bleachers where there were about twenty-five children who were "Axel's friends." The kids would cheer whenever the Little Rascals came on. They would laugh at Axel's jokes, and they would appear stumped by his riddles. Then, at the end of each program, Axel would take a microphone taped to a three-foot stick and ask if the youngsters would like to say hello to their family or their friends out there in TV land.

One day when Axel asked this question, a little boy who looked about seven-years-old shot his hand up in the air. Axel poked the microphone in front of him, and the camera came full-face on the youngster. "Vat's your name?" Axel asked.

"Jimmy," said the child.

"And vat vould you like to say?"

At first, Jimmy said nothing, he simply grinned. Then suddenly he made a certain vulgar hand gesture directly into the lens of the camera and said, "This is for you, Herbie, and I really mean it!"

Immediately the TV screen went dark, and it remained that way for two or three minutes. When the show finally reappeared, Axel was interviewing the other kids and telling jokes and asking riddles. Jimmy was nowhere in sight. There was not even an empty spot in the bleachers where Jimmy had been sitting moments before. No one mentioned Jimmy or what he had done. It was as if Jimmy had vanished from the earth. It was as if Jimmy had never existed. That is the core of Lindvall's memory—not what Jimmy had done, but the idea that a person could disappear without anyone saying a word about it.[22]

If our friends fail to mention our loved one who has died, it can hurt us deeply because we wonder how a person who was so special to us can be forgotten so easily. Most likely it will be incumbent on us to bring up the name of our loved one in conversation with others because the great majority of people are uncomfortable with death and avoid mentioning the subject.

The degree to which people are uneasy with death was driven home to me several years ago when I was working closely with young people. I had planned a sex education unit for our congregation's senior high youth group. Thinking that some parents might be uneasy about their child's involvement with the program, I mailed a letter in advance to all the parents. I described the program so that parents could decide whether or not they wanted their child to participate. I heard from no one, and the unit went off as planned. A few months later I mailed a letter to our senior highs telling them that we would be looking at the topic of death for the next couple of Sundays. I received three telephone calls from nervous parents inquiring about what exactly I planned to do. They had no problem with their children talking about sex, but they were uncomfortable with the topic of death. Such is our world today.

If someone close to you has died, you know what a wonderful treasure it is to have people share with you their beautiful memories of your loved one. A few friends will take the initiative to share these memories with you in a conversation or a letter, but others will not. Many people are afraid they will upset you, and thus they avoid the subject altogether. You must take the initiative with people, asking them to share their memories of your loved one. Be sure to probe them for the heartwarming moments and the funny stories they remember. These will produce tears of joy in you.

Cherished memories of a loved one do not prolong the grief process; instead, they help us proceed toward acceptance and hope. Native Americans have a beautiful saying: "How can the dead be truly dead when they are still walking in my heart?" Although our loved ones may no longer be physically present, they continue to touch us through our cherished memories. And when someone shares a story about our loved one that we had never heard, it adds to our treasury of remembrances and awards us with a special blessing.

Accumulating a cache of memories aids our healing. Remembering the beautiful ways our loved one contributed to the well-being of others diminishes the intensity of our sadness. However, we must do more than simply reminisce. We must also move forward with our lives.

✢

Live a Rich Life!

A few years ago a good friend of ours died. Connie was fifty years old when she discovered a lump in her breast. The lump proved to be malignant, and the surgeon removed it. Unfortunately, the cancer had already spread to other areas of her body. She underwent radiation and chemotherapy for slightly over a year before she died.

Death is rarely easy to accept, but some deaths are more difficult to accept than others. We have the capability of sending space probes to Jupiter that transmit photographs back to earth. We can send electronic mail to any country on our planet in a matter of seconds. We are able to track people's movements from satellites circling the globe. We can determine a person's DNA from the back of a postage stamp that was licked months before. Knowing that it is possible to accomplish such incredible feats makes it all the more difficult for us to accept the fact that there are some things we simply cannot do—such as preventing cancer from taking the life of our loved one before she has grown old. Goodness knows that the medical community and Connie's family and friends did everything humanly possible to prevent death from taking her. However, in the face of this insidious disease, we all became powerless. Connie herself alternated between denying it and fighting it, but it was not a fight that could be won. Perhaps in a few years scientists will uncover the clues that will provide a cure for cancer and the disease will be overcome. However, we have not yet reached that point. All of us are still waiting for a medical breakthrough.

Why did Connie, like so many others, develop cancer? No one knows. Perhaps she accidentally ingested some cancer-causing agent; perhaps she had a defective gene; perhaps it resulted from environmental pollution, or a yet undiscovered virus. It is highly unlikely that we will ever know the answer. However, we can state with confidence that God did not want Connie, or anyone, to develop cancer. God is a God of life who wants the best for all his children, and God does not go around giving people terminal illnesses. It is not God's will for people to get cancer. Since God's love for us knows no end, I believe that God's heart also broke when Connie died. God's heart broke for all the additional beauty and goodness that Connie had not yet spread, and God's heart broke for her husband, her children, and her parents because God knows what it is to lose a child.

Death may enter our lives at any time; it will not wait until we find it convenient. Thus, it is essential for us to spend the time we have wisely. How will we live our lives following the loss of a loved one?

The retired seminary professor Fred Craddock tells a story about one of his seminary classmates. The man served as a missionary to China and lived there for a number of years with his wife and two children. One day, without warning, soldiers appeared at their front door and placed the family under house arrest. For several days they had no idea what would become of them. Then unexpectedly the soldiers came and said, "You have been cleared to return to America." The whole family celebrated! The soldiers interrupted their celebration with instructions. They would be allowed to take no more than two hundred pounds with them.

The family had been stationed in China for many years and during their stay had accumulated a number of possessions. It would be a challenge for them to decide what to take and what to leave behind. They lugged out the scales and began to disagree over the value of various items. The mother said, "We must take this vase. It's precious, and we will never find anything like it again." The father replied, "Don't forget, this is a new typewriter. We have to include it." They kept placing things on and off the scale, figuring and refiguring what they would be able to take with them. Finally they worked it out, precisely two hundred pounds. They informed the soldiers that they were ready to leave. The soldiers asked, "Did you weigh everything?" The father replied, "Yes, we did. We have whittled it down to two hundred pounds exactly." And then the soldiers asked, "Did you weigh the children?" The mother and father were stunned. "Well, no, we didn't." One of the soldiers snapped, "You have to weigh the children, they count too." And in a split second the typewriter and the vase and everything else simply became trash. None of it seemed so important after all.[23]

Often in our lives we forget what's genuinely important until something jars us. Too often in the routine course of our lives we find ourselves being distracted by things that are not that critical in the big picture.

Although we would never wish for a painful tragedy, sometimes it holds precious lessons for us. A crisis often exposes all the clutter and nonessentials in our life and reminds us of the things that are genuinely important. A painful loss can remind us of what is worthy of our time and energy, and what is superfluous.

On several occasions people who experienced a tragedy in their lives have shared with me how their crisis opened their eyes and helped them to rearrange their priorities. They became aware of the many ways in which people in our society spend their time involved in activities of little importance, while failing to involve themselves in matters that are meaningful and fulfilling.

After suffering the loss of a loved one, some people struggle through each day because they never quite move beyond feeling sorry for themselves. They use their self-pity to cut off significant ties with others and to fend off feelings of joy that might seep into their lives. They remain sorrowful and lonely, their character deteriorates, and people find them unpleasant to be around. However, some people refuse to let their pain and suffering be the end of their lives and are actually motivated to seek a more fulfilling existence. Rabbi Harold Kushner is a good example of someone who has contributed much more to the world following a terrible personal loss. Rabbi Kushner's son, Aaron, was born with progeria (rapid aging) and died at the age of fourteen. Rabbi Kushner could have become embittered with life and spent the remainder of his time on earth feeling sorry for himself. Instead, he used the insights he gained from his tragedy to help others. His book *When Bad Things Happen to Good People* has helped millions of people in this country and abroad. If he were given the choice between having his son back and writing an international best-seller, he would choose in an instant to have his son back. But in this life we are not afforded the opportunity to make such choices. The choice before

Kushner was, Now that your son has died, how will you live the remainder of your life? He has chosen to live it to its fullest.

What about you? Have you experienced a loss so devastating and so painful that you feel as if your life is finished? You may believe that all meaning and purpose have been drained out of your life and that there is little reason to carry on. It is *not* true. Life will continue. In the widely quoted words of Yogi Berra, "It ain't over till it's over." You simply have no idea what lies ahead of you.

No matter what tragedies come your way, you must hold on to the hope that God will be with you to help you through the pain to a better day. God will strengthen you despite your feelings of weakness and fatigue. When Dr. Elisabeth Kübler-Ross was doing her research on dying patients, she went from room to room in the hospital interviewing people at the end of their lives. She was attempting to figure out what people were experiencing internally—every mood, every feeling. At some point she began to notice that some of the patients she visited were particularly tranquil. They were much more at peace than others. In addition, she noticed another pattern: These patients were tranquil shortly after a particular maid had cleaned their room. Acting on a hunch, she stopped the maid in the hallway one day, and asked, "What are you doing with my patients?"

The maid became frightened and defensive, responding, "I'm not doing anything with your patients." Dr. Kübler-Ross continued, "No, I mean this in a good sense. You're helping them. They're calmer after you have been there. What are you doing to help my patients?"

The maid replied, "I've had two babies die on my lap. It hurt so deep I could hardly stand it. But even in the midst of my pain, God did not leave me. You know, God lost a son too. And God gave me strength. That's what I tell them. God will give you strength."[24] When you feel as if you have exhausted your will to go forward, you can discover in God the strength you need to persevere.

Further, God will present you with new possibilities for a rich and meaningful life. However, God will leave a momentous decision up to you. In the end, you alone must decide how you will live the remainder of your life. You may choose to live it in despair, or you may choose to live it in hope.

Although this decision is yours alone to make, you must avoid isolating yourself from others as you strive to regain meaning and hope in your life. You may feel as if you would rather not be around other people for a while, but you must push yourself to overcome this temptation. The fact is, you need other people to assist you during your difficult times. You need your family, and you need people beyond your family.

Last year, less than one week before Christmas, I conducted funerals for two men in our congregation who had died unexpectedly. One man had a cerebral hemorrhage; the other never regained consciousness following heart bypass surgery. It struck me that in their grief both widows made the same remark to me: "I don't know how people make it through something like this without a church." This comment has been made to me numerous times over the years. When people face the loss of a loved one, they recognize their need for a group of concerned friends who will help them, and they recognize the importance of their religious faith. Active participation in worship heals our souls. We have a deep, internal need to be fed spiritually. We need to pray with others and to hear the words of Scripture that have spoken to people for centuries. In addition, we need to listen to music that touches us in ways that words cannot.

If you have a community of faith, strengthen your ties. If you are not an active member of a congregation, find one where you can become active. The church declares that in the person of Jesus of Nazareth, God became most fully known to us. God's Spirit flowed through Christ as through no other. Following the death of Christ, the community of faith was called by God to carry on Christ's mission. The church is now the body of Christ in the world, and the love of God flows through its members. In his letter to the church in Galatia, the

Apostle Paul wrote that the members of the body of Christ are to "bear one another's burdens." That is, fellow Christians can help shoulder your load when it has become too great to manage alone. God's Spirit can work through the household of faith, gradually healing your wounds and eventually replacing your despair with hope.

In the early days of your grief, genuine hope may elude you. Your extreme sadness may so overwhelm you with despair that it clouds your vision and renders you incapable of imagining anything hopeful. Before you are capable of reaching the point where your faith produces hope, faith may simply give you the strength you need to endure the intense pain that engulfs you. During extreme moments your faith may amount to little more than hanging on by your fingertips as you search for answers. If you have been stunned by a tragedy, you may encounter a crisis in your faith. You may find that the old pat answers no longer ring true. Those beliefs that served you adequately while life went smoothly may sound hollow and trite. However, this is not the time to abandon organized religion. Instead, involve yourself in a vital congregation where the members are honest enough to readily admit they do not possess all the answers and are open to discovering new ways of understanding God and the life God calls us to live. A caring community of faith that exudes an atmosphere of loving concern and openness to your spiritual struggles provides a rich environment for personal healing and spiritual growth.

In addition, a community of faith is a wonderful place to find a meaningful way to express your faith through service to others. Earlier I mentioned the importance of letting people do nice things for you. In addition, you need to do helpful and loving things for others. When we are hurting, if we are only recipients of care from others, we may begin to think and act like helpless victims. Doing something for someone else helps us to know that we are able to give as well as receive. It's critical to know that other people need us and that we can make a positive impact on the life of another. If you have lost a loved one, you know how much it means to have people come by the house for a visit, to receive a note from someone who has you in her thoughts and prayers, to have someone fix a meal for you and drop it by your home. If you know how much these things mean, you can do these things for others.

There are countless opportunities for service to others. The widow of Reggie Morris (the friend I mentioned in the first chapter who died of a brain tumor) joined with several other members of our congregation to create an after-school tutoring program. For several years, she and the others have shown up every Tuesday and Thursday afternoon to work with low-income third-graders from a nearby elementary school who are at risk of falling behind their peers. In addition to helping her third-grader with basic math and reading skills, she communicates her love and concern to her student, enhancing the child's confidence. She is having a very positive impact on the life of a child, yet she continues to say, "I do it because it helps *me*. I'm sure I get more out of it than my student."

The widower of Connie (the friend I mentioned in the previous chapter who died from cancer) and the mother of Erica (the twenty-one-year-old who died suddenly) have also made great strides in their healing by remaining involved in the church and living their faith by serving others. Active participation in a religious community is an essential piece of the healing process.

✥

Conclusion

Over the course of my ministry, my beliefs about God and the world have undergone significant changes. These changes have evolved as a direct result of my struggle with unjust suffering. In this book, I have shared the answers that help me understand the various reasons for suffering. However, making sense of our suffering is not all we must do. In addition, we must discover how to live our lives fully despite the personal tragedies that occur to us.

The world is an amazing, yet imperfect, place. Despite the fact that God has no desire for tragedies to wreck people's lives, no one is guaranteed immunity from suffering. Because our loving God is not an all-controlling God, bad decisions, accidents, defective genes, and natural disasters generate untold anguish. How else could it be in an interconnected world where genuine freedom exists, and where creation is an ongoing process?

Despite disasters that strike us, it is not inevitable that they crush us. Life is not ultimately despairing because God's love for us is measureless. When pain enters our lives, it not only pierces *our* core, it penetrates the very heart of God. Touched by our suffering, God moves to lighten our burden by sharing the weight of our grief and giving us needed strength to endure.

While we are free to respond to our pain however we choose, God urges us to strive for the best possibilities given our circumstances. God cannot magically reverse the events of history or make all sorrows disappear, but God can lead us toward our best possible future.

Moreover, God inspires other people to bring healing into our lives. They may be fellow sufferers or patient listeners. They may bring a comforting word or help point us in a new direction. Their support—like God's —is crucial to our renewal.

When tragedy strikes and the ties with a loved one are severed, many believe that the pain will never lessen and meaningful life is no longer feasible. However, the transforming power of God makes new life possible. This new life does not deny the pain of the loss nor ignore the void that will always exist, but it embraces the hope that the current pain can lessen and joy can return.

It is our faith in God that makes possible a meaningful existence. Paul's words at the conclusion of the eighth chapter of the Letter to the Romans provide a powerful and succinct statement of our greatest hope. He declares that there is nothing in the universe—not even death—that can separate us from God. Thus, despite the deep wounds and losses we suffer in life, we are able to find the needed strength in the One who continues to create heaven and earth. And since the God of the universe makes possible new life in our present existence and in the life yet to come, we are challenged by the following question: How can we best live in ways that bring honor to our deceased loved ones? *Challenge yourself with this question as you begin each day,* and you will discover that a rich life is still possible.

NOTES

1. I learned of this golf course from a sermon by Dr. Richard Hershberger titled "A Box of Chocolates," preached at Westminster Presbyterian Church, Oklahoma City, Oklahoma, August 21, 1994.

2. Diogenes Allen, *Christian Belief in a Postmodern World* (Louisville: Westminster/ John Knox Press, 1989), 2.

3. Burton Z. Cooper, "When Modern Consciousness Happens to Good People," *Theology Today* 48, no. 3 (October 1991), 291.

4. From a sermon by William Sloane Coffin entitled "My Son Beat Me to the Grave," reprinted as "Epilogue: Alex's Death," in *The Courage to Love* (New York: Harper & Row, 1984).

5. John Calvin, *Institutes of the Christian Religion* (Philadelphia: Westminster Press, 1973), 204.

6. *Institutes of the Christian Religion*, 208.

7. From a sermon by G. Renee Ahern entitled "Palms of Passion," reprinted in *Biblical Preaching Journal* (Spring 1993), 5.

8. From a sermon by Thomas G. Long entitled "The Disciples' Final Exam," preached on July 7, 1991, at Fifth Avenue Presbyterian Church in New York City.

9. Charles Birch, *A Purpose for Everything* (Mystic, Conn.: Twenty-third Publications, 1990), 94.

10. *A Purpose for Everything*, 92.

11. From a sermon by Clyde Fant entitled "The House Where Freedom Lives," delivered on July 4, 1991, at the Interpreting the Faith Conference at Union Theological Seminary in Richmond, Virginia.

12. From a sermon preached on March 5, 1995, on the radio program *The Living Word*, by the Reverend Bob Russell, pastor of Southeast Christian Church in Louisville, Kentucky.

13. The story of Larry Trapp was adapted from a transcript of the story presented on National Public Radio's *Morning Edition*, July 29, 1992.

14. Anne Lamott, *Traveling Mercies* (New York: Pantheon Books, 1999), 42.

15. Bernie Siegel, *Love, Medicine, and Miracles* (New York: Harper Perennial, 1986), 217.

16. *Love, Medicine, and Miracles*, 219.

17. As told by the Reverend John R. Claypool in a sermon published in the *Biblical Preaching Journal* (Spring 1990, Volume 3), 23.

18. From a sermon by Dr. Joseph B. Mullin entitled "Go-go, Slow-go, No-go!" preached at First Presbyterian Church, Greensboro, North Carolina.

19. Amy Hillyard Jensen, *Healing Grief* (Redmond, Washington: Medic Publishing Co., 1980), 10.

20. C. S. Lewis, *A Grief Observed* (San Francisco: Harper & Row Publishers, 1961), 66.

21. Harold Kushner told this story in November 1996 while speaking to a forum at the Jewish Community Center, Richmond, Virginia.

22. Michael L. Lindvall, *The Good News from North Haven*, (New York: Pocket Books, 1991), 22–23.

23. From a sermon by Fred Craddock entitled "Have You Ever Heard John Preach?" published in *Best Sermons: 4* (San Francisco: Harper & Row Publishers), edited by James Cox.

24. From a sermon by Thomas G. Long entitled "On Having Angels for Dinner," preached in November 1992, at First Presbyterian Church, Richmond, Virginia.

✢

About the Author

If you would like to contact Dr. Jones for speaking, or if you have a personal story you wish to share with him, you may contact him at his Web site:

www.gregoryknoxjones.com